Rescuing Jeffrey

Rescuing Jeffrey

....

RICHARD GALLI

ALGONQUIN BOOKS OF CHAPEL HILL   2000

Published by
Algonquin Books of Chapel Hill
Post Office Box 2225
Chapel Hill, North Carolina 27515-2225

a division of
Workman Publishing
708 Broadway
New York, New York 10003

Published simultaneously in Canada
   by Thomas Allen & Son Limited.
Design by Bonnie Campbell.

The names of some of the persons depicted
in this book have been changed.

Library of Congress Cataloging-in-Publication Data
Galli, Richard.
     Rescuing Jeffrey / by Richard Galli.
       p. cm.
     ISBN 1-56512-270-4
     1. Galli, Jeffrey,—Health.   2. Spinal cord—
Wounds and injuries—Patients—Biography.
3. Spinal cord—Wounds and injuries—
Patients—Rehabilitation.   I. Title.
RD796.G27 G35 2000
362.1'97482'0092—dc21
[B]   99-089826

10 9 8 7 6 5 4 3 2 1

FIRST EDITION

A small flake alone—
delicate and innocent.
But a group—hell bent.

JEFFREY GALLI,
DECEMBER 1997

Rescuing Jeffrey

....

Depend upon it, sir, when a man knows he is to
be hanged in a fortnight, it concentrates his
mind wonderfully.—SAMUEL JOHNSON, FROM
JAMES BOSWELL, *LIFE OF JOHNSON*

....

Prologue

....

I BELIEVE IN A WORLD OF CHANCE, OF GOOD LUCK AND
bad luck.

But sometimes chance hits so hard, it takes our breath
away. When it hits that hard, *when chance hits that hard,* it
feels as if the sun and the stars are exploding, and all the
laws of nature are spinning out of balance, and there is
nothing solid or real anymore to hold on to.

On July 4, 1998, the sun and the stars spun out of balance in a backyard swimming pool in Barrington, Rhode
Island. My son, Jeffrey, a likable teenage boy just starting
to enjoy life and get a grip on it, dove into the pool, struck
his head, and nearly drowned before being "rescued" by
his parents into hopeless quadriplegic paralysis.

This is the story of how a family—my family—first
cheated death and then flirted with death over the next ten
days. Because the story is told primarily from my private

thoughts and memories, it is nothing more than a glimpse of one father coping with the ruination of one son. The story is neither universal nor emblematic. It is not political and it may not be instructional. It is just a story. It describes the process I went through to resolve my own predicament: *I had brought my son back to life, and then I had to find a way to kill him.*

Saturday, July 4

....

IT WAS EARLY EVENING ON JULY FOURTH. THEY CALL IT Independence Day. It was still light and warm. Our family was at a small party. I was just finishing my second brownie.

One of the kids came up to the house and told us Jeffrey was in the pool, underwater, and not moving. It was only a joke, of course. Jeffrey was just goofing the other kids. He was underwater, holding his breath, having fun. Absolutely.

My wife, Toby, left the house to check. She rushed. Parents have to do that. As I got up from my chair to follow her, I made a face, a signal that some people might be suckered, but I knew better: this was a joke. Even knowing it was a joke, I hurried out the door. Parents have to do that.

At the pool's edge, Toby was a step ahead of me, blocking my view. I expected to see Jeff paddling in the water with a half-ashamed, half-elated smile. He wasn't. Toby shouted "Jeffrey!" once, and jumped into the water. As she cleared from my view, I saw Jeffrey and jumped in.

Jeff was near the bottom of the pool. He looked restful. He was facing up, his arms and legs spread slightly, comfortably positioned. His eyes were open.

Toby began raising him to the surface. I grabbed him and pulled harder. As he rose into my arms and I saw his face, I thought, This is really happening.

Jeffrey's lips were dark blue. His tongue was distended and dark blue. His eyes were wide open, the pupils huge, unmoving, staring into nothing, like the eyes of a fish on ice.

We heaved the upper part of him onto the concrete apron, and I jumped out of the pool. I grabbed one of his arms and pulled him clear of the water.

My son had become a heavy, limp, dragging thing. When last I had seen him, a few minutes before, he had been seventeen years old, nearing six feet tall, wonderfully fit, and handsome.

We rolled Jeff onto his back. I put my hands together on a spot below his chest and pushed several times, quick and hard. I bent over his face to start breathing for him. His mouth was open wide, but his dark blue tongue was in the way. It was so distended, so huge. It was like a cow's tongue. Even more than the eyes, the tongue affected me. I didn't know that about drowning; I didn't know about that color blue and the bloated tongue.

I put my right hand over Jeff's mouth, covering the

slimy blue tongue and lips. I put my left hand on Jeff's forehead and his hair. Then I began breathing into his nose. The passageway was clear, and the breath went in without resistance. As I whooshed the air into his nose, I could just see his chest rise as his lungs filled. When I lifted my head, I could see his chest settle back. I did it again, and again. After a few repetitions I found a rhythm.

I remember someone screaming and people forming a circle around our little drama. Four couples were at the party, and among them were three people with medical degrees. I remember one of them telling me Jeff had a pulse. Another told me I ought to clear.

Clear. I was glad to be reminded. I had to clear the mouth and throat for Jeff to breathe. I fumbled with Jeff's mouth. His big blue tongue had retreated, but now Jeff's teeth were clenched together so tight that I could not move them.

I don't need to do this, I thought. I have a passageway already: his nose. I don't have to clear his mouth. Ignore his mouth. Get back to work.

Chunks of mucus came out of Jeff's nose. I wiped it away and began to breathe through the nose again. Once or twice, between breaths, Jeff seemed to hiccup slightly, and more mucus came out. Not much. One of the doctors helped clear away the mucus and cradled Jeff's head.

For a while, as I breathed for Jeff, his eyes remained wide, fixed, and lifeless. But slowly, magically, his eyes began to reawaken. The lids closed just a bit. The pupils got just a bit smaller. And then the eyes started to move.

Jeff's eyes began to circle, circle, searching for a place to land. As I saw Jeffrey coming back, reacting, doing anything but lie there in a lump, I stopped breathing into him for a time and pounded on his chest. "Come on, Jeff," I said, "come on."

The process continued: Breathe in, rise, and watch Jeff's eyes. Breathe in, rise, and watch Jeff's eyes. His pupils jerked from place to place. At any other time, at any other place, the look in Jeff's eyes would have sickened me. So lost they looked, so empty. But at least they were moving; that was a start.

The doctors reported that Jeff's pulse was strong. I kept breathing into him.

Eventually some police arrived. They said an ambulance was on its way. I kept breathing into Jeff. A few minutes later some emergency medical technicians appeared. They called instructions to one another: Get this, get that.

Our little crowd was now crowded. At any moment I expected someone to push me aside. I could see equipment being staged, arranged. I paused for a few seconds, looking for a professional replacement. When no one jumped in, I continued breathing into Jeff.

The air went in so easily. Easier than blowing up a balloon. Almost as easy as a whistle. I think—I am not sure now—but I think a small part of me wondered why Jeff had not yet coughed, gagged, retched fluid. They always do that in the movies and on TV. They always cough just before waking up.

When the EMTs were ready, they let me know. Someone crouched down next to me, I moved to the side, and my place was wordlessly taken. I got up, moved back a step or two, and stood next to Toby. Now my eyes, from the greater distance, could see more of Jeff. He was no longer blue. His eyes were only half open. He was alive.

When we had pulled him from the water, he seemed dead already. Now he was alive again. I thought, We did it. We brought him back to life.

I lifted my left hand and held it up to my eyes. It's a thing I do to check my composure. If my fingers are shaking, I know I am nervous. If I can will my fingers to become settled and calm, then I can become calm myself.

Standing there while the EMTs worked on my son, I looked at my fingers and was surprised. They were absolutely still. Granite fingers. I wasn't nervous. How could that be? I tried to show Toby. "Look at this," I said, holding out my hand. How curious.

This was the reason; it must have been: From the instant we saw Jeff, we had a job to do. Lift, push, drag, breathe, pound, breathe again and again and again. Do this first, then this, then this. I was too busy working on Jeff to despair of losing him. And now the job was done, and Jeff was alive.

IT WAS AT this moment that I heard one of the EMTs say to another, "Get the blocks. We have to stabilize his neck and head. There may be damage to his spine."

And hearing that, I thought, My God, what have we done?

Into the System

Jeffrey was taken by ambulance to Rhode Island Hospital. Toby rode with him. She was given the only passenger seat. Michael Goldstein, our good friend and party host, was a psychiatrist—a doctor—and was therefore permitted to accompany Jeffrey in the body of the ambulance. Without a medical degree, I followed in the car. My clothes were soaked. The ambulance drove very fast. Around corners, it tipped so far I half expected it to crash. I could see through its rear windows. It was brightly lit, and I could see one of the attendants working, talking.

At the hospital, Toby, Michael, and I were put in a small room. One of the staff explained that Jeffrey was being stabilized and evaluated. We waited. Eventually one of the trauma doctors appeared, and as Toby and I held hands, the doctor told us what we had to know.

"I'm sorry, but it doesn't look very good," the doctor said. "Jeffrey hit his head, and he fractured some bones in his cervical spine. Unfortunately, it was a very high break, and it injured his spinal column. Jeffrey is paralyzed from his neck down."

"This is my son!" Toby shouted, and collapsed on the couch. I remained standing, listening to the doctor. I thought for the second time that day, This is really happening.

"Your son can't breathe on his own," the doctor continued. "We have intubated him, and we are going to use a ventilator to help him breathe. In a little while you can see him. But it's too soon right now; a lot of people are in there working on him. It's a pretty busy place right now. We'll bring you in as soon as we can."

We spent another half hour in the room. Gradually, the center of our family's life was moving. Our home was in transit. Earlier that afternoon, our home had been in East Greenwich, Rhode Island. We used to live in a salt-box colonial on Cindyann Drive. Before the night ended, we would live in Providence, on the second floor of the Hasbro Children's Hospital, in the pediatric intensive care unit. I could feel it happening.

People came in to talk to us. A social worker. Then a Catholic chaplain. He was very nice and very smart. He offered only a few words of comfort, and he did not mention God or faith or prayer. In fact, now that I think of it, he didn't say much at all. He was smart enough to be practically silent. He was patiently, earnestly silent. He was not there to talk; he was there to listen if we needed to talk ourselves.

Gradually, we were processed into the medical system. The trauma doc came back to give us a more detailed appraisal. Jeffrey was, at least for now, a quadriplegic. He could not move anything below his neck. He could not feel anything below his neck. We could not take him home. Jeffrey would probably never walk again, never feed himself. We could not take him home. Tubes were being put into his trachea—the channel to his lungs—so that a machine could breathe for him. Jeffrey would probably need a mechanical ventilator for the rest of his life. We couldn't see him yet. In a little while they would be ready for us. We should be prepared for a shock when we saw him. He was unconscious. He was paralyzed. He was seventeen. He was young. Miracles could happen. The first twenty-four hours would be important. If he were going to improve, it would probably happen in the first twenty-four hours. We shouldn't lose hope. But we could not take him home.

When we finally went in to see him, Jeffrey was on a gurney. Plastic tubes—one thick, some thin—were slithering into his mouth. The mechanical ventilator hissed. Jeffrey was trapped, like a fly in a web, fed upon by plastic and metal. Gauges flickered. Things beeped. Jeffrey looked dead; only the equipment seemed alive. A network of wires and intravenous tubes latched onto Jeffrey's body, his arms, his groin, like worms or snakes . . .

No, that's wrong. I shouldn't think of it that way. I shouldn't get metaphoric about it.

Jeffrey was alive. He was lying on a gurney. He was being kept alive by smart, well-trained, compassionate people, using the tools that other smart people had made for just this purpose.

I could have thought of it that way, but I did not.

I resented the process. I resented the machines. I resented the fact that strangers were using machines on my son. Just a few minutes before, when a woman had told Toby and me that we might not be able to see Jeffrey, I resented it, and said, "Under what circumstances would we be prevented from seeing our son?" Of course, she relented immediately. But I resented someone taking custody of Jeffrey and treating me as an outsider. And now I resented the fact that he was lying there, hooked up, connected, plugged in like an appliance.

An hour after the accident, Jeffrey lay on a gurney, a passive recipient of medical services. He was fully enrolled in the system, which would work miracles and preserve his life. And I resented it.

My son had become the hospital's patient. They had to keep him alive; that was their job. I had to be his dad; that was my job. My clothes were still wet. I began to wonder, Can I help them keep him alive and still be his dad? Can I do both of those things?

Waiting for the Miracle

As Jeffrey was being moved to the intensive care unit, Toby and Michael Goldstein and I made our way to the nearby "family lounge." We were joined by Beatrice and Bob Swift, who had been at the party with us. While I was breathing into Jeff, Bob Swift had tilted his head to improve the airway and had helped me clear the mucus from Jeff's nose. At the hospital we hugged, cried, and slumped. I don't remember a word any of us said, but I have a clear picture of Beatrice Swift's eyes as she sat next to Toby. Her eyes were bubbling with tears, but her eyes were not soft. They glowed, they bore into Toby like lasers. I have never seen so much compassion mixed with so much force, as if Beatrice were trying to make it better by willing it to be so.

To the extent any news came to us at all, it was unremittingly harsh: This was a very bad fracture, very high.

The prognosis was worse than grim. No one mentioned the possibility of improvement without using the word miracle.

During the first twenty-four hours, as Jeffrey lay waiting for his miracle, the medical staff told us what to expect. Jeff would be stabilized in the intensive care unit. Doses of steroids would help suppress inflammation, which, if unchecked, would further damage his spinal tissue. He would get an MRI exam to better evaluate the extent of the injury. He would be tested to confirm their suspicion that his spinal injury was "complete"—that no function remained below the point of the break.

He had some rectal tone; that was a good sign. His head would be set into a "halo"—a device to hold his head and neck bones in rigid alignment. He would probably never move without a wheelchair, never breathe without a ventilator. He would need twenty-four-hour care for the rest of his life. But he would almost certainly survive. No one knew how long he had been underwater. No one knew if he had suffered any brain damage. But he was alive, and they could keep him alive. They could keep him alive, and if he were lucky, someday he could move his head from side to side.

A surgeon looked me in the eyes. He practically commanded me to see the positive side of things. "You saved your son's life," he said. I stared back at him. What do you know about my son's life? I thought.

AT SOME POINT, Toby, Michael, and I drove to East Greenwich. We took care of our dog, Kirby. Jeffrey was unconscious and paralyzed, but Kirby needed a walk and a meal. Toby grabbed a few things, and I took a shower. Had I been offered the choice, I would have stayed in the shower until now, and I would be there tomorrow too. We drove two cars back to the hospital.

....

I'm walking around in a Zombie state thinking about you and your family. I try to imagine this nightmare happening to me, and when the pain gets too intolerable, I snap out of it. But this is not something you can do and I weep for you.

—RISA GUTTMAN-KORNWITZ

....

Sunday, July 5

....

I SLEPT ON A COUCH IN THE FAMILY LOUNGE THE FIRST night. With many interruptions during the night, Toby slept on a reclining chair in Jeffrey's room. We stayed in the family lounge or the intensive care unit the next day, except for brief intermissions. Early Sunday morning, I drove to my parents' house, sat in their kitchen with a towel on my head, and told them that their grandson was a quadriplegic. They said they would call the family. I told them we wanted no visitors. I thought visitors would be a hindrance, that we had too much to do and no time to waste.

Toby's sister, Ida Schmulowitz, was commissioned to tell their mother, Jeanne, about the accident that morning.

Toby went to visit her mother later in the day, as soon as she could.

Our friends immediately took charge of Sarah, Jeffrey's fourteen-year-old sister. She stayed with the Goldstein family the first night. The tragedy had hit the four Galli and Goldstein teens first of all. Annie and Noah Goldstein were in the pool or on the apron with Sarah when Jeff made his dive. The kids experienced the bewilderment when he did not surface, and they were first to become alarmed. They learned together that life can be a fragile thing, but that relationships need not be. That first night, rather than fleeing the scene of the accident, Sarah tucked herself into the Goldstein family and was sustained.

The Wave

As soon as the first rush of action was over, people came to visit us. I thought that I could keep them at bay, but I could not. First thing Sunday morning, Toby called her rabbi, Les Gutterman, who came as soon as he could.

Toby, Jeffrey, and Sarah are all Jewish, members of Temple Beth-El. Les is warmly supportive of whatever the hell I am. Les was going through his own family medical crisis at the time, but as he sat with Toby and me and focused on us, you might have thought we were the only two people he knew in the world. He asked a few gentle questions to learn our situation. He got us to talk.

He listened for a while, didn't say much at first, and then when there was a pause long enough to warrant it, he said, "There is going to be a wave of love that is going to sweep over you. It's going to happen, and you have to accept it."

I didn't know what he was talking about. Toby told me later neither did she. A "wave of love"? I wasn't that close to anybody. The thought of love breaking over me like surf wasn't even attractive, much less plausible.

A short while later, Toby got a call from one friend, who told her that another friend felt absolutely compelled to come to the hospital right away. Toby said okay. She also asked Rebecca Goldstein to bring Sarah to the hospital. Sarah was afraid to come into the hospital; she was afraid of seeing Jeff. Toby said she would meet Sarah outside or in the lobby, but that Sarah ought to come, even if not all the way.

When word came that Sarah was in the downstairs lobby waiting, Toby and I went down to see her. The lobby seemed to be full of our friends. Several couples in their forties and early fifties, with whom we had been birthing and raising children in sync for the last two decades, had converged. The sight of them struck me like a blast from a fire hose.

That was just the start. People came quickly, in flocks, en masse. An ever-widening circle of anguished friends was drawn to our new world at the ICU. The mothers, the fathers, the couples—the parents—came to us and cried with us. In the Sunday paper, there had been a short article. Teenager injured in pool mishap; in critical condition. The story spread quickly by word of mouth.

Before I continue with this story, I have to say something about the crying. There was a lot of it. It was pervasive and unpredictable. Every new face could bring an eruption of tears. Every memory could bring torrents. Over the next few days I could be reduced to puddles anytime. Huge, heaving, powerful sobs of despair. Everyone cried. Trust me. So, as the story continues, whether I mention the crying or not, you'll just have to remember that the stage directions are pretty consistent: Toby cries; Richard cries; the doctors all cry.

In the Hasbro Hospital lobby that morning, with all these comfortable faces around her, Sarah was finally convinced to go upstairs and see her big brother. Jeff was unstable, a mess in every respect. The staff was constantly responding to crashing emergencies, loud alarms. It was the worst time for Sarah to see him. But Toby did not know if Sarah would ever see him alive again and didn't want Sarah to miss the chance.

Over the next few weeks, Sarah became a gypsy, moving from home to home and family to family. She spent her weekdays at day camp. Nights and weekends she spent at movies, malls, and concerts and—as often as could be expected—in the hospital. Her hosts made all the arrangements; we had to plan nothing at all.

During most of Sunday, Toby and I shuffled between Jeffrey's intensive care room and the family lounge. Jeffrey was heavily drugged and utterly encumbered by machinery. He was a vessel full of drugs, shock, and nervous system injury. He was barely recognizable. The flesh of his face was red, furrowed, oily. He didn't seem like much of a platform on which to build a future.

As new people arrived in the family lounge, we would

tell them what we knew. We quickly became clinically adept at explaining the situation. It was not enough that our son was paralyzed and unconscious a few feet down the hall. For our own world—our friends and family—Toby and I became the primary source of information on the subject. We became very precise and very plainspoken about exactly how emphatic was the destruction of our son.

Everyone grieved, and everyone offered hope, at least their own version of it. Some hoped for a recovery, even if only partial. Others hoped for a cure, even if late in coming. Some others hoped for the strength or wisdom to live a full life within a limited body.

As our friends offered us their hope, I saw in their eyes not confidence but hunger. Only because they felt the need for hope so much did they have any to offer us. But I now spoke in a new dialect. The word hope had not yet been defined for me. I did know, for absolute sure, that it meant to me something different from whatever these people had in mind.

I began to sense that hope and life were for these people transcendently related terms. These people hoped Jeffrey would live. So long as Jeffrey lived, they told us, there was hope. Life meant there could be hope, and hope meant there could be a life worth living.

I took no comfort at all from any of their hope. I could hope for Jeffrey to walk again, just as I could hope to be singles champion at Wimbledon some day. Without a foundation in fact, without information to form a basis for hope, to me it was nothing but wishing in the wind.

The best I could hope for was the ability to do my job. I was Jeffrey's dad. I hoped to measure up to that responsibility. I hoped to be strong enough to think clearly and act decisively. Given what the doctors had told me, all I could realistically hope for was to learn what I needed to learn and to make the decisions I needed to make.

Like a driver in a skid on a high-speed highway, I knew an accident was happening and hoped only to steer for the best collision.

....

We pray that the doctors and the best medical science
will offer him a healing recovery. We wish you faith,
and courage, and strength in the days ahead.
—MARION GOLDSMITH

....

Option Two

In the bowels of the hospital, shielded from vulnerable electronic equipment, the magnetic resonance imaging machine is kept. To get a set of MRI scans, a patient is fed into a huge magnet. The output is a set of small but detailed images, each representing a cross section or slice of the body. I had seen MRIs before. To see the details inside a few inches of cervical spine would take dozens of images.

While we waited for the scanning to be completed, Jeffrey's pediatrician appeared. A wonderful, sensitive, compassionate man, Dr. Stuart Bodner seemed very far out of his element. Infant earaches, colds, and flu—these were his stock-in-trade. But Jeffrey was a quadriplegic swallowed by a magnet, and Dr. Bodner seemed no better able to accept that than we were.

He arrived to comfort us at exactly the worst time for him. I was boiling, looking for an available medical target. Dr. Bodner appeared and was elected.

"Everyone tells us about Option One," I said to him. "They tell us a lot about Option One. He goes into the system. He gets put in a wheelchair. He gets put on a respirator. He stays that way forever. Why is no one asking us about Option Two?"

"What is Option Two?" Dr. Bodner asked us.

"Option Two is we terminate our son's life."

I blindsided this guy. It was horrible, what I did to him. He had come here to lend a shoulder to cry on. Not for this.

I wanted to know: Why was the staff avoiding the question? The question was there; it had to be answered. Why were they avoiding it?

Leaving the hospital a head on a neck on a vent in a chair is not a good outcome. Why was the hospital acting as if it were the *only* outcome? Whatever we might eventually decide, why were they not talking to us about the possibility—the possible choice—of withdrawing Jeffrey's life support?

"You can't do that," he said. His usually soft voice was practically shrill with bewilderment. The idea was causing him pain, not anger.

"Of course we can," I replied. "Jeffrey is a minor; we are his parents. The hospital's policy—which is posted on walls—is that any patient can refuse medical treatment. We are the people who make that decision."

"But you can't just decide to kill him, not when he's in this condition," Dr. Bodner said, as if the issue were obvious, beyond dispute.

"Why not?" I asked.

"Because he has a viable, living brain," the doctor said.

The Enemy Shows Its Face

A few minutes later, Jeffrey was wheeled from the MRI room. The doctor who had supervised the test came out to talk to us. He was a stranger. I asked to see the MRI scans, and he complied without hesitation. He shuffled through an envelope of films and pulled out the one that even an amateur could comprehend.

"This is the spinal cord," the doctor said, pointing to an area just south of the cranium. "And this is the contusion of the spinal cord."

It was a round, wispy puff of ghostly gray, like a charcoal cotton ball.

"What is a contusion?" I asked. In my former life as a litigation lawyer, handling personal injury cases, I had used the term many times. Suddenly, in my new life as a quadriplegic's father, I didn't know what the word meant at all. Not really. Not when so much depended on *exactly* what it meant.

"It's a bruise, something like a black-and-blue spot," he

said. "If you smash your hand with a hammer, the tissue remains, but it has been compressed, squashed, destroyed."

The *contusion*. I had finally met the enemy, the cause of Jeffrey's ruination. That spot. That contusion. It looked harmless, no more lethal than a whisper of smoke.

....

Jeffrey is a great kid and he is lucky to have you
for parents . . . You will endure and make
the right decisions because you have what it
takes. Follow your hearts, your instincts.

—KATHIE STREICKER

....

Monday, July 6

....

I ASKED TOBY TO TAKE A WALK WITH ME. I HAD SOME-
thing to say, and I wanted to say it outdoors, out in the
world beyond the hospital. Long before, when I asked her
to marry me, I did so in a letter. It was 1969. As I wrote the
letter, I was sitting on dirt in the dark outside a barracks at
the Fort Dix army base.

Now it was 1998, and Toby and I were about to have the
most important face-to-face conversation of our lives. Just
as we had in 1969, we were reaching out to each other in an
atmosphere of love, responsibility, and dread.

We went outside. It seemed to be a nice afternoon. We
sat on a concrete wall. "We have to talk," I said to Toby. Just
trying to get those four words out, I completely broke
down. I had been holding the words back for hours. I
knew what I was going to say. I was pretty sure Toby knew

as well. As clearly as I could under the circumstances, I stated my case.

"We can't let Jeffrey get caught up in the system," I said. "This place, these people, they all have one thing on their minds: keep him alive. You know how it is. They have skills and they have to use them; they have machines, and they have to use them. Once Jeffrey is surrendered into the system, they will own him. All their decisions will be automatic. First this, then this, then this."

"What are you saying?" Toby asked.

"I'm saying that there are decisions to be made. We have to make them. Just because these people can do things for him, it doesn't mean they have to do those things. We have to remember: This is not just anyone. This is Jeffrey. We have to do whatever is best for Jeffrey. Do you understand what I am saying? I am saying we may have to kill our son. We have to consider that option. The hospital won't consider it. We have to."

For a while, all Toby could do was watch me cry. It was not something she was accustomed to. For a while I let myself be helpless and surrendered to grief.

I am not often paralyzed by indecision. For whatever reason—genes, experience, training, whatever—I have learned to make decisions when I have to make them and live with the consequences, good or bad. While I enjoy being intuitive and emotional, I trust most the rational side of things. I like tools and devices. I like to know how things work and how to make things work. I like projects. I don't like hysteria.

During the earliest part of the crisis, when tension was

acute and the need for action immediate, the part of me that is able to calculate and plan ahead *just somehow did so.*

For example: back at the swimming pool, as I jumped into the water to follow Toby, my left hand instinctively reached into the pocket of my shorts and flipped my wallet backward toward dry land. Later, as I was about to follow my near-dead son to the hospital, some partition in my memory opened and reminded me, Get your wallet; and there it was. Safe, dry, ready for use. How practical.

Perhaps it would have been easier for me as a parent to be totally spontaneous, to give Jeff love and tears and let others perform their professional duties. I just couldn't do that. I just could not be that way. Back at the pool, while I breathed air into my son's limp body, a project had been given to me: the disposition of Jeffrey's life and future. I felt accountable for everything that happened to him, every action taken, every decision made. I shared the responsibility equally with my wife, of course; but I think I realized the weight of it more vividly than she and certainly earlier.

The Argument

Less than two full days after the accident, as we sat on the concrete wall, I asked my wife to consider whether keeping Jeffrey alive was something that people who loved him ought to do for him. Like a lawyer summing to a jury at the end of a trial, I reminded Toby of what we already knew.

The argument—even then I recognized it to be a rhetorical proposition—went this way: Jeffrey was a wonderful boy with a great heart. He was shy. He could be charming. And he had also been a troubled kid. Over the past two years, his reasonably bright mind had gradually fallen under a cloud. He seemed to be receding from the world, disconnecting from his peers. He dropped behind in school. He couldn't do his homework. Simple assignments—a short essay or book report, for example—could take weeks instead of hours to accomplish. He would start, hit a wall, and then give up, overcome by frustration and anger.

He stayed up late every night. On weekends he would sleep until noon or later. He withdrew from the family in a painful way. Fights would erupt over nothing: doing dishes, doing homework, walking the dog. We parents worried terribly. Everything we tried ended in argument, division. We still had good times, but they were becoming rare.

Although we knew he had friends, none of them ever came to our house. He almost never visited their homes or did anything with them after school or on weekends. When I offered to take a vanload of kids to the ski slopes up north, he would decline. Although we knew he liked girls, he didn't go on dates. He didn't go to dances. He went to movies often, but alone.

In his junior year, Jeffrey was flunking half his classes. For a long time he combated all of our attempts to help. He would take care of the problem himself, he insisted. He would just try harder and do better, he promised. But he had fallen too far behind, and as he began to appreciate that, it only made him more despondent and more dark.

Jeffrey knew, by the middle of his junior year, that he was crashing. By December 1997, it was truly coming apart. He had a short assignment for English that was overdue. I told him he had to complete it, whether or not his teacher gave him credit. I told him he had to learn that responsibility could not be evaded forever. On Christmas Day we collided. Working on the assignment—or at least making a show of it—Jeffrey stared at a computer screen for hours, doing virtually nothing but glowering. I sat at a computer right next to him, editing a book as a favor to a friend. I told Jeffrey if he didn't finish the project by that afternoon, the family would go to a movie and dinner without him. He just stared. He was still staring at the screen as we left.

Hours later, when we returned, Jeffrey was gone. So far as I could see, he had not written a word. It was a dark, clear night. His bike was missing from the garage. I waited. Then I drove to the nearby movie complex. His bike was not there. I drove home again. He was still missing. I began driving back and forth from home to the theater, taking different routes. It was possible he had been in an accident. The main route to our house goes by a memorial to Timmy Lyons, a youngster killed by a hit-and-run driver a couple of years ago. I went by it often that night.

As I searched for Jeffrey, I began to consider the real possibility that something horrible might have happened to him. I called the police. They said no one had been reported injured that night; they said they would watch for Jeff and asked me to keep them informed.

I began to drive more slowly. I would hug the side of each road, poking my headlights into the bushes and ditches. A few times—when I saw a metallic glint or a strange shape or shadow—I got out and checked more closely. I went back to the house and shut off all the lights. Each time I completed the route from home to theater and back again, I would check the house, hoping to see that one of the lights had been turned on.

By about two o'clock in the morning—long after the theater had closed and its parking lot had emptied—I began to think that an accident was now the most probable explanation for Jeff's disappearance. And as I prowled the streets, I was no longer simply excluding the possibility of an accident. I expected to see Jeff lying there. And I began to imagine a world without him.

At about half-past two, I came home. After a minute or two, as I stood in our back hall, Jeffrey appeared out of the dark. He said he had gone to two movies. When he came home, he had left the lights off. Jeff probably expected me to chastise him, but I could think of nothing useful to say. While he watched me, I called the police, told them he was safe, and thanked them for their concern. Then I went to bed. Jeffrey had not died that night. But I had become acquainted with the possibility.

Eventually, we all began seeing a psychiatrist and a therapist. Jeffrey's diagnosis was "major depression." Jeffrey did not resist being given a diagnosis. The psychiatrist explained to Jeffrey that he—like lots of other teens—could use some help. Exercise, diet, drugs, and discipline—he was responsible for it all. The intervention worked. Jeffrey agreed to try medication. He used it faithfully. He attended regular meetings with a therapist. Jeff hated what had been happening to him and wanted to fix it.

Once the medical and therapeutic systems were in place, our school system also responded. We worked out a plan to reverse Jeff's tailspin. Two of his courses were dropped. Accommodations were set up, including extra time for him to complete exams.

Over the next few weeks, things improved for Jeffrey. Little by little, he was brightening. He made progress in school. He had his driver's license, and now he used every imaginable excuse to get behind the wheel. He would take a short drive almost every night, like a dose of medicine. I had a very nice car laid up with a broken transmission, and we began to put it back together, piece by piece.

By the end of the spring semester, things were still not perfect at home, but they were a lot better. They were only as tough as things are supposed to be with teenagers, and that was fine by me.

In the few days before the accident, things really began to come together. Jeffrey was going to summer school, not because he had to but because he wanted to; he was committed to doing well. Rather than try to cram the necessary credits into his senior year, Jeff agreed to spend an extra year in high school to give himself a chance to prove that he could excel.

Jeff was looking hard for a summer job. We completed the rebuild of his car. The transmission was put back together—with only a couple of pieces left over—then heaved up into place with considerable grunting and cursing. Jeff and I got dirty and sweaty together, but when the key was turned, the car awoke. The transmission was notchy, but the car ran like a colt in springtime, quicker than it had ever been before.

I told him I would not register the car until he had proved that he deserved it. Four days before the accident, Jeff drove his bicycle ten miles in a horrible rainstorm to get to class by 8:00 A.M. I registered and insured his car immediately after that. Jeff obtained a note from the school, certifying that his grades were enough to earn him a "good student" insurance discount. When he handed me the form, he had the kind of look on his face that a young boy might have if he had just been awarded the Nobel prize.

On Saturday morning, July Fourth, I taught Jeff how to change the oil and filter on his car. He had already mounted both his bike rack and his snowboard rack. It was July, the middle of summer, a hot day, and my son had mounted on the car a snowboard rack that had never been taken out of its box in the two years since we bought it. The previous winter had been so dark and cheerless, Jeffrey had not gone snowboarding even once. Now he was getting ready for a run down a mountain months before the first snowflake would fall.

Suddenly, magically, my son was taking pleasure in his life and making a future, *and he knew it.* He was excited, happy, confident. He was making plans. He was getting ready to have fun again. For the first time in two years, maybe more, we could see in Jeffrey's eyes and smile the kid we used to know.

Jeffrey drove to the Goldstein's party. His mother told him to drive slower. I sat in the front seat next to him, enjoying his enjoyment. I remembered what it was to be young, with a wheel in my hands. I was happy to see him share the same boyish pleasure.

In his dark days, Jeffrey never would have come with us to the Goldstein's party. That he came at all—what a surprise. It was as if he were saying, Look at this; I'm back.

It was probably an expression of joy, Jeffrey's leap into the swimming pool. He had worked so hard for the right to make that leap.

....

Guy and I are thinking of you both . . . Our children are all so precious, and we know how much you all must be hurting.—PATTI SHAFFER

....

As Toby and I sat on the concrete wall on Monday, outside the hospital where Jeffrey lay, we carried in our hearts a picture of our son that no one else could possibly know. No kid deserves to break his neck. But if it had to happen to this particular kid, did it have to happen at that particular moment in his life?

I was nearing the end of the argument.

"Jeffrey didn't live in his mind," I reminded Toby. "If I broke my neck, maybe I could spend my days reading Hemingway and Faulkner. But not Jeffrey. He needs to move. He needs to do things.

"The doctors are going to save his life. And for the rest

of his life, he will be nothing but a head and neck, sitting in a wheelchair. Is that a future Jeffrey would want us to build for him? Would he choose that life?

"He will never be able to run or walk. He will never be able to use his hands. He will never be able to move under his own power. He will be dependent on others for practically everything he needs or wants to do for the rest of his life.

"He will never put his arms around a girl and hug her, kiss her, or dance with her. He knows what sex is, but he will never be able to experience it the way he dreams about it. He will never be able to drive a car. He will have to watch as all the other kids grow up and have the kind of life he has lost. He will have to watch as his sister, Sarah, grows up, goes to dances and on dates, and grows into the life that he has lost.

"We are his parents," I said to Toby. "Nothing is automatic. The system can put Jeffrey into that kind of future, but we have to decide whether we should let them do it.

"And I don't think we should let them," I said. "I think we may have to stop them, and soon. I don't think we can save our son's life. I don't think Jeffrey would want us to. I don't think he could stand it, living that kind of life, day after day, knowing how much he has lost. I think the pain would be unbearable, and it would never go away."

We hugged each other. Actually, she mostly hugged me, since I was hunched over weeping buckets.

"The worst part is this," I said. "All of his life, he will think that he did this to himself. He jumped into the pool himself. No one pushed him. He did it to himself. After all his screwups, just at the moment when he had turned it around, just exactly when he finally had a chance to be proud of himself, he goes and screws up again.

"It doesn't make any difference if that's true or false," I said. "That's what he will believe. It's his fault. He did it to himself. That's what he will think. All his life.

"I can't stand the thought of him living with that kind of pain," I told my wife. "We can't let it happen to him. We can't."

I was blubbering. Toby put her arm around me.

"I love Jeffrey so much," she said. "I just don't want to see him in pain."

Toby didn't say much while we sat on the wall. Later, she told me what she had been thinking.

She was worried that no matter how hard we tried, we could not take care of Jeffrey. That someday, possibly soon, he would end up in an institution. She was also afraid that her judgment would be clouded by selfishness or divided loyalty. Whereas I was concentrating on one victim, she told me later, she saw two: Jeffrey was the first, and I was the second. To her, I seemed so radically altered that her fear that I might take my own life was equal to her sorrow over what had already happened.

She didn't want to lose Jeffrey, and she didn't want to lose me or the family we had built. She wanted to save our relationship. The salvage job she had taken on was bigger than the one I had. She wanted to save everyone. She sensed that my focus, being so narrowly aimed at Jeff, was sharper and more reliable—that my tunnel vision would make me unselfish.

She was, of course, wrong. There was not then, nor would there ever be, a second when personal interest was out of the picture. For Jeffrey, I wanted the best outcome and believed that to be death. For myself, I wanted to destroy his paralysis, to get it out of my world, to fix it, to conquer it. I was greedy to loosen its grip on Jeff, on me, and on the whole privileged world in which we lived before paralysis intruded. Jeffrey's death would be a victory over his paralysis. I was that selfish. Luckily, I knew it and could try to minimize its impact on the decisions I made.

A philosopher once said that a man is his acts. A man is defined by what he does. When I said Jeff might have to die, Toby trusted me because she mistakenly thought I was unselfish. I trusted myself because I knew just how selfish I could be and fought to act otherwise.

We talked about the reaction, how our family and friends would react if we let Jeff die. Some of the people we considered one by one. Toby's mother, Jeanne. Her sister, Ida. My parents. Our daughter, Sarah. Everyone.

"I can take the heat," I said. I paused. "That's why I signed him into the hospital. That's why I signed the authorization for treatment. I knew we might have to have this talk. I knew how this might end."

I absolutely wailed. Having held the anticipation of this moment in check for two days, I gave in to the luxury of an agonizing release. Any stranger passing by would have heard me and would have marveled at how tenderly that striking woman was managing that hysterical old man.

"I try to think of a way out of this, but I can't. I can't. I try to believe that helping Jeffrey live is the right thing to do, but I can't believe it. If I were in his position, I know what I would want him to do for me. And I know I should do the same thing for him. I know it. I'm sure of it.

"I keep thinking," I told Toby, "that I'm going to have to kill him myself because they won't let me do it the right way.

"This is not going to turn out well," I told my wife. "This is not going to have a happy ending."

The Decision

The talk on the wall on that Monday took about forty minutes. By the end of it, we had come to terms with our intentions: unless we could be convinced otherwise, we were going to withdraw Jeffrey's life support. A few hours after breathing life back into him, I was prepared to take his breath away. And I had begun lobbying for that result.

The fact that Toby agreed with me helped convince me that the decision was correct. But her concurrence also made the decision awfully *real*. Before, Jeffrey's death was hypothetical, theoretical. Now it was a plan, a goal, an objective.

Before, I had been overcome by sadness and despair. Now I was overcome by a colder, more sinister feeling of dread. Suddenly, I had to manage this horror. I had to accomplish this task, when all I really wanted to do was find a hole and retire.

We had made our decision conditional. Less than two days had passed since the accident, and a reasonable window for dramatic improvement had not quite closed. Jeff's condition was still unstable, and that meant it could be transitional. He could get better.

As we dried our tears and walked into the building, Toby and I were changed people. We loved our son. We wanted him to live. But if we had to do it, we would let him die. And now we had to deliver that message.

·····················

We know that time must be standing still for you now, and we can only try to imagine what your days are like, but we would like you to know that we are here thinking and worrying about you, hoping for the best.—ROBIN KERN

·····················

In the early hours after the accident, Jeffrey was so much less than himself. He lay absolutely still in his marvel of a bed. The bed could be raised and lowered and could be made to twist on its axis, side to side. It was an elaborate, massive, and expensive cradle. Everything worked electronically, with buttons and switches, as would Jeffrey for a long time.

His body had been laid out on the bed in almost exactly the same position we had found him in at the bottom of the pool. Jeffrey's head was in the halo, a heavy black band of graphite that encircled his head. Four stainless steel bolts were set through the halo. The tips of the bolts were sharpened, and they were torqued through Jeffrey's skin into his skull. Around his chest, Jeffrey wore a stiff plastic vest with a lining of artificial wool. The vest was made tight with thick leather belts. Connecting the vest and the halo were four thick black graphite rods. Each rod had two adjustable sockets, one at the halo end and one at the vest.

A neurosurgeon had fitted the halo vest. Once the alignment of Jeffrey's skull and neck bones was exactly right, the surgeon clamped the four rods in their adjustable sockets. In this way, Jeffrey's head, neck, and chest were all immobilized, made rigid, in their most favorable position.

And in this way, the only muscles and joints that could respond to his will were made effectively paralyzed as well. People could bend the leg he could not feel, but he could not move his neck, which ached to be turned and stretched. Jeffrey was to be locked in the halo vest for at least several weeks, possibly several months.

Jeffrey's face seemed to have collapsed upon itself. He seemed flushed, as if in constant fever. He was heavily sedated. He was drugged to sleep intravenously. He came out of sleep only when the drugs tapered off.

He could not talk. A thick, ribbed, plastic ventilator tube filled much of the right side of his mouth. He couldn't close his teeth without compressing the tube and sounding an alarm. A couple of smaller tubes followed the fat vent tube down his throat.

His mouth was open all the time. His jaw was not slack; it wanted to close. But his teeth and lips had been forced apart by the plastic tubes. His lips had become cracked and chapped. The intravenous lines gave him all the fluid and nutrition his body could use, but the IVs didn't wet his lips and tongue. Jeffrey was constantly thirsty, and he could not drink.

The hospital provided sponges to wet his mouth and lips. The sponges were small, set on the end of thin plastic sticks. Toby used them more than I did.

She would dip the sponge into a cup of ice water, then dab Jeffrey's lips, moistening them with droplets. Because his lips were so chapped, she would not rub them with the sponge. She would simply deposit drops onto his lips.

Jeffrey's tongue would reach out for the sponge. Jeff's tongue had developed its own personality. His tongue crinkled, it bent, it cupped the sponge and slowly drew the sponge into his mouth, seducing the sponge for its faint caress of water. The process became sensual. Jeffrey's eyes closed as his tongue drew the sponge inside.

"It's the only thing we can give him to make him feel better," Toby once told a friend. "And I love to give it to him. I love to give pleasure to my son."

....

Sometimes life doesn't seem fair—these things shouldn't be happening . . . Never give up hope because medicine has come a long way and we do believe miracles do happen in strange ways. —LINDA MITTLEMAN

....

Monday afternoon, while I was out running an errand, Toby met with Dr. Francois Luks, one of Jeff's surgeons, and Dr. Linda Snelling, medical director of the Hasbro PICU (pediatric intensive care unit). Toby informed them that we were considering removing Jeff's life support. They talked about whether Jeffrey should be actively involved in the decision. The doctors thought he should be. Dr. Luks was crying, according to Toby.

People kept coming to visit us. Rabbi Gutterman came back. Another of Jeff's pediatricians—Sue Pakula—also came. People brought us sandwiches, drinks, fruit baskets, cookies, and themselves. By Monday afternoon, some people were making their second or third visit. The parents' lounge at the Hasbro PICU was turning into a Galli family annex. Sometimes, when I entered the room, before taking up a conversation I would ask if there was a quorum.

There wasn't much to report. Jeff's condition had not changed. There was no improvement. There was no good news. He was still alive, our friends would remind us. We should be thankful for that.

They began to tell us about the outside world. People were talking about us, asking about us. People who knew us well would get calls from people who knew us less intimately. Close friends were drawn to us, compelled to visit us. Others were compelled to make contact but didn't want to intrude. So instead of calling us, they called our friends. Two days after the accident, we who had known nothing about paralysis had shared our new wisdom with our friends, who were now being called on to educate the next ring out.

Suddenly, we all had a hunger for information. Visitors brought us magazine articles about paralysis, pages off the World Wide Web, or just gossip about medical developments hazily described and poorly documented. Had we heard about the laboratory rats with surgically severed spines who were given drugs and could walk again? Had we heard about the quadriplegic whose arms and legs came back ten years after his accident? Had we heard anything new or positive? What had we heard? Some people wanted to know; others, having done homework of their own already, handed us a page or a folder full of pages, hoping it would help.

Toby and I hugged our friends, talked about Jeff's past, his accident, and his condition; but we did not tell them about Option Two. I promised myself never to lie to our friends about what choices were laid before me, but I also never recruited anyone to consider the choices with me. We told our friends what the hospital staff told us about Option One, which always ended with Jeffrey's leaving the hospital, going to another hospital for rehabilitation, and returning to live with us, if possible. We never asked our friends to share the agony of the other option we were considering, minute by minute, and consequently we never invited them to argue against it.

Dry Tears

Jeffrey was engaged in a frantic struggle against his plastic tubing. The system that delivered air to his lungs filled his mouth and throat, chafing and choking him. No air was coming past his vocal cords, so he could not talk. When he cried, he was silent. When he asked questions or called for help, no sound came out. His lips were contorted and chapped. The plastic tubing had become the awful focus of his world. In effect, Jeffrey was being raped.

Sometimes he tried to bite the tubes, to break them. Alarms would sound as his air was cut off. Sometimes he would grip the tubes in his teeth and try to work them out of his mouth, a millimeter at a time. But the tubes were held in place by strong fabric tape. If he managed to move the tubes so much as half an inch, the stretched tape would just pull them back.

Jeffrey's world was filled with noise from machines he couldn't see. His body was numb from the neck down, and from the neck up he was in pain. When he was not unconscious from his medication, he was either slowly rising into consciousness or crying to be put to sleep again.

In this condition, gradually over the first two days, Jeffrey had to learn that he was a quadriplegic. He had to learn that he was not ever again going to use the arms and hands and legs he could not feel.

I remember the first time I told him these things. "You were in an accident," I said to him. "We were at the Goldsteins' house on the Fourth of July. You jumped into their swimming pool. You hit your head."

He nodded yes. He moved his head no more than a quarter of an inch, but he was nodding, as if to say, Yes, I remember.

"You broke some bones in your neck," I told him.

"Am I paralyzed?" he asked, forming the words slowly, but without sound.

"Yes," I said.

"Can I use my legs?" he asked.

"No," I said, "you can't use your legs. You can't walk."

His face reddened and he scrunched up his eyes to cry —I expected an eruption—but only one or two tears came out. Maybe it was from the medication, some kind of fluid imbalance. I don't know. But he couldn't manage more than a tear or two.

His lips trembled around the tubes. His half-opened

43

mouth wailed silently. After all, he had no air to cry out loud. He wanted to talk but could not. He wanted to cry but couldn't do that either. If we held his hand, he couldn't feel it. All we could do was stroke his hair and his cheeks and hope that it might help.

ALMOST EVERY TIME Jeffrey woke up, he had to learn about his accident as if for the first time. He would rouse out of his medicated sleep, disoriented. He would ask what had happened. He would be eased into understanding. He would eventually remember the accident, at least part of it. And then he would be reminded—but to him it was news each time—that he was paralyzed.

Each time, he would cry. His lips would curl around the tubes, a tear would form at the corner of his eye, and he would silently cry.

The first time I talked to him about the accident, Jeffrey had all he could take when he learned he would not walk again. He didn't want to know any more. I comforted him as best I could.

"Jeffrey," I said, "you are not your legs. Jeffrey is not in your legs. Jeffrey is up here." I tapped his head. "Jeffrey is up here, and that means you are still here, all of you." I leaned over him and nearly touched his nose with mine as I looked into his eyes.

"Last week, when you moved from the den to the kitchen, you used your legs. Next time you move from the den to the kitchen, you will use a wheelchair. But you will still be moving from the den to the kitchen, and it will be under your own power."

He heard me, and he seemed to understand. But he didn't want to understand. He didn't want to know any more. No more legs? It was worse than that? He didn't want to know. He knew too much already. He said he wanted to go to sleep. He wanted drugs to go to sleep. He got them.

No More Hoops

Eventually, the intravenous drugs were tapered off, and Jeffrey was forced to wake up again. We spoke about the accident and his paralysis. He once more asked if he would ever walk again. I told him the doctors were not hopeful that he ever would.

"What about my arms?" he asked me.

"You won't be able to use your arms," I said.

"No more basketball?" he asked.

"No more basketball," I said.

Enough. Stop. No more. He knew too much. It hurt to know that much.

Sometime later, we went over the same thing. No legs. No arms. And then, his eyes looking straight into mine, he said, "No driveway basketball?"

"No driveway basketball," I said.

Let me peel back another layer of this story. I was overweight and out of shape. Early in 1998, during Jeffrey's dark days, I decided to install a small basketball court at our house. I believed—possibly fantasy at the time—that if Jeff and Sarah and I could spend time together shooting hoops, I would get thinner and the ties that bound us

45

would get stronger. So we planned a landscape project that included a half-court basketball zone off the new driveway. We measured a local court to get the right size. Jeff and I laid out some rough designs for the project on my computer. We hired a landscape contractor, who made the plan more realistic. After much searching, I ordered a wonderful pole-and-goal system (well built, adjustable, with a Plexiglas backboard) from a company I had found by searching the Internet.

The pavement for the driveway and the court was laid in June, and a couple of times Jeff and I went out and spent a few minutes just dribbling and passing, imagining the first game. The hoop system arrived at the end of June. It was in the garage, in several heavy boxes. It was loosely scheduled to go into the ground the week after the Fourth of July.

On Friday, the third of July, I got impatient. I was tired of thinking about basketball but not playing any. "How about shooting some hoops on the downtown courts?" I asked my kids. Jeff said sure; even Sarah wanted to do it. So on Friday the three of us went to a municipal court and swatted the ball around. We played cutthroat, one on one on one. Jeff easily beat me, although I put on a meaningless surge at the end to make the score respectable. Sarah didn't score at all, but she got in there and mixed it up. It was a great outing. Soon it would be a regular part of our life.

The next day Jeffrey broke his neck.

A couple of days after the accident, when my son said to me, "No driveway basketball?"—well, we both knew what he meant. With his whole wrecked future spread out in front of him, he had the heart to miss a game we had never had a chance to play on the little court we had never gotten a chance to complete.

In the days following Jeff's accident, I began to have fantasies about our basketball hoop. On Monday I called the landscaper to put a stop to the project. But I thought constantly about the hoop. Should I go ahead and install the hoop? Should I let life go on that way? Could I ever play there? Could I play with Sarah and not with Jeff? Would it be fair to Jeff if I did? Would it be fair to Sarah if I did not? Could I shoot the ball alone? Could I do that? And if Jeffrey died?

Maybe . . . maybe what I should do, I thought, is donate the stuff to the high school: lay down the pavement and install the hoop system Jeff and I were going to use. I imagined a brass plaque: IN MEMORY OF JEFFREY GALLI. I imagined that some days, when the pain of memory got to me, I might go down to the high school and shoot a few on Jeffrey's court.

My fantasizing would get mixed up. When this court was built and dedicated, would Jeffrey be alive or dead? If he lived and came home, would the hoop be a sign of hope, a motivation for him? Or would it depress him because other kids were using it and he was not? Should I erect the hoop at home or at the high school? Should I send it back to the manufacturer? Should the plaque be brass? Would thoughtless kids deface the plaque and spray graffiti on the court?

Memories of the Future

Quadriplegic paralysis steals legs, arms, hands, fingers —and the future. Jeffrey's paralysis stole our future. We looked into each other's eyes and said, No more driveway basketball. We could have gone on: No more snowboarding. No more car, with the new plates and the transmission we had patched together. No more . . . well, no more anything we had ever dreamed of. Because no dream included paralysis. Not one.

Set dreams aside. Dreams aren't real. Few people see their dreams come true. Let's not talk about dreams. It wasn't dreams we were losing. It was real life we were losing.

No *concept* of the future included paralysis. No high school graduation or senior prom. No Saturday afternoon golf. No meeting the first steady girlfriend. Those aren't dreams. Those are real things. But don't think so big. Think smaller. No more taking out the garbage or mowing the lawn. No more driving to the store for milk. Think smaller still. No more urinals or toilets? No more solid food? No more scratching an ear or blowing a nose?

Jeffrey's accident struck him like a bomb as he was crossing the bridge to manhood. He was approaching independence. He probably had some idea what a summer job, a weekly paycheck, and a set of wheels might mean in his life. He probably had some faint notion of the freedom he would know at college. No matter how grand his expectations, I knew they were too small.

Jeffrey was about to have his own life. Over the course

of about one year, he would be preparing to leave his parents in his wake. It was natural and foreseeable and universal, and it was something I had done myself. I looked forward to watching Jeffrey do it. He had passed through the years when we parents decided everything in his life for him. He was almost all the way to the point where he would make every meaningful decision on his own and we could only hope to be consulted from time to time.

At the hospital, I began telling people, "This is when he's supposed to be saying 'Screw you, Dad'—not 'Please.' I didn't want to hear how the accident would bring Jeff and me closer together. He had the right to grow farther apart. Dependency isn't love or friendship. Dependency is the need that love or friendship can never quite fill.

Now Jeffrey would rely on his parents more than he had done when he was a baby lying in his crib. In place of an independent future, filled with possibility, we had to consider how his nose would be blown and his urine contained.

Jeffrey had seen his future, had it in his grasp, took it with him as he drove to the party, and had it tucked inside him as he dove into the pool. He had the memory of that future even now, as he lay limp in his hospital bed. The memory of the future would last forever, but the future itself was gone.

Death destroys the future, but it is polite enough to wipe out the past as well. If I die today, I won't be around to remember what my expectations were as of yesterday. Paralysis is not so nice. It ruins the future, but it leaves intact the memory of all your expectations. Jeffrey would have plenty of time to consider *exactly* what he had lost and *exactly* what might have been.

....

I am praying for you, for strength and for courage. If good thoughts could heal, all would be well.
—RUBY SHALANSKY

....

In the first few days after the accident, we had to say so much to Jeffrey, and it was so hard. Jeffrey had no voice. We had to read his lips. But his lips were chapped, and his mouth was stuffed with tubes. He would slowly form the words with his lips. We would strain to read them. He would strain to form the words. He would exaggerate each vowel and consonant. We would go one word at a time. "Is the first word *water?* Is the first word *what?* Are you asking a question? Are you asking for water?"

Often, we would have to use the alphabet: "Jeff, I'll go through the alphabet, and you blink when I hit the right letter. A B C D E F—" *Blink.* "Is it F? Okay, I'll write down F on this pad. Now, let's do the second letter."

It was tedious. It was painful. It caused Jeff physical pain to communicate around the tubes in his mouth. But he fought to communicate because it caused him even greater pain to be mute.

One day, shortly after he awoke, he let me know we ought to talk. I grabbed the pad and began the process.

"A B C D E F G H I—" *Blink!* I wrote down an I on the pad and showed him.

"A B C D E F G H I J K L M N O P Q R S T U V W—" *Blink!* I put down a W.

"A—" *Blink!* I wrote down an A.

"A B C D E F G H I J K L M N—" *Blink!*

"A B C D E F G H I J K L M N O P Q R S T—" *Blink!*

"A B C D E F G H I J K L M N O P Q R S T—" *Blink!*

"A B C D E F G H I J K L M N O—" *Blink!*

"A B C D—" *Blink!*

I knew where this was going. He had spelled out "IWANTTOD . . . "

"Jeffrey, do you want to die?" I asked him.

He closed his eyes and nodded yes.

I put my hands on his cheeks, touched his nose with mine. "Jeffrey," I said, "listen to me. You could have died in that pool. We brought you back to life. If you had died in the pool, you and I could not be talking to each other now. We would not have had these days together. Isn't that important? Aren't you glad we can be with each other now?"

He nodded yes.

Maybe I am lucky and he really was glad to be with me. Or maybe he said it just to comfort me. As I was trying to comfort him. After all, outside his room, I was saying something entirely different.

So long as Jeffrey was alive, it was important to talk him out of dying. I knew that shock, drugs, and depression would wreck his power to think rationally about the future. It was our job—Toby's and mine—to think rationally about the future. It was Jeffrey's job to think *optimistically* about the future, at least until he was well enough to think realistically one way or the other. So when

51

he first started telling me he wanted to die, I was not willing to believe him.

At one point I asked him, "When you go to sleep, do you want to stay asleep and never wake up, or do you want to wake up again?" His eyes widened. "Wake up," he said. That time I could clearly read the words as his silent lips formed them, pushing against the tubes.

Wanting to live, wanting to die. Sometimes wanting one, sometimes wanting the other. These were not decisions Jeffrey was making. He was simply a kid *wanting*. To the extent he wanted the nothingness of death, it was certainly only a reaction to the fact that at present he couldn't get anything else he wanted.

Into a Hotter Fire

By Monday the balance of Jeffrey's life had pretty much been determined. He had shown no improvement in function since the accident. The first, most important "window of opportunity" had closed. Two of his doctors asked to meet with us.

Ken Burnett was a neurosurgeon who had been instrumental in keeping Jeff alive, and Linda Snelling was the medical director of Hasbro's pediatric intensive care unit, where Jeff was staying. They arrived at the parents' lounge together. Les Gutterman was already there, and he stayed with us. Toby and I knew this was going to be an important session.

The doctors gave us their assessment, most of which we already knew. Jeff was a "high quadriplegic." His fractures were at the C1-C2 level—the very top of the spinal column, just below the cranium.

"It's as bad as it gets," Burnett told us.

Jeff had shown no improvement since the accident. He was incontinent and could not breathe on his own. The tubes running into his mouth ought to be replaced. Jeff would need a tracheostomy. Surgeons would cut a hole low into Jeff's neck and install a plastic tube that would connect through hoses to a mechanical ventilator. Eventually, with training, Jeff might be able to speak again. Really speak, with a voice, not mutely with his lips or by choosing letters one at a time.

We could expect his body to get smaller. He would lose muscle and mass. Skin sores would be a lifelong problem. Loss of skin integrity could be followed by infection.

Jeffrey would need lifelong, round-the-clock care, the doctors told us. Someone would have to be near him always, to respond immediately if the ventilator broke down, or a tube popped off, or the buildup of mucus in his lungs needed suctioning. Jeff would need an alarm system for his ventilator.

Jeff's fractured neck bones had to be fixed. One way, the doctors said, was to fuse the vertebrae surgically, using bone grafts and steel hardware. That would get Jeff out of the halo in about a month. The other way was to wait and see if the bones fused naturally, without surgery. It would take about three months in the halo for that to happen—if it could.

On the upside, natural fusion—if it worked—would leave Jeff with the maximum possible residual movement in his head and neck. On the downside, it would delay some of the things that a rehab hospital could offer him. Jeff might have to stay in a kind of limbo for weeks: not quite in intensive care, but not fully engaged in rehab either.

We were not asked to make the fusion decision that day, but it would have to be made soon. The doctors also made clear that we had to choose a rehabilitation hospital soon. They suggested a hospital in Braintree, Massachusetts.

Then they told us about blood clots. His circulatory system was in disarray. Clots could form and could kill him. Some doctors recommended surgery to implant blood strainers; others did not. Something else for us to consider and eventually decide.

"What about Option Two," I asked them. "We have not yet talked about removing his life support."

As well as I could, I tried to explain to the two doctors why we had to consider all of our options, even the one that they would never have mentioned on their own. Most of all, I tried to explain to them who Jeffrey was and why the path they had laid out for him might not be the way to go. I gave them the argument: What kind of kid Jeffrey was. How far he had fallen. How quickly he had climbed back up again. How awful was the timing of this accident.

We were not trying to make a decision for all kids or for all quadriplegic kids. We were trying to make a decision for our kid. And so far, we were finding it impossible to see our kid living at peace in the world for which the medical staff was preparing him.

Rabbi Gutterman had his arm around Toby's shoulders. She was so glad he was there. He was such a comfort to her. Perhaps it was the link to her sense of tradition, or perhaps a comradeship in sorrow; whatever it was, Les gave her things I could not offer at the time. A skirmish had started, and I was engaged.

Ken Burnett seemed to have the greater difficulty discussing Jeffrey's death. Burnett seemed in pain, frustrated, and a bit confused. He was certainly uncomfortable. He was a fine doctor. We had been lucky to have him. He took good care of Jeff, and he had helped us to learn what we needed to know. When he had spoken about medical treatment, he was on familiar ground, in charge. Now I was talking about killing his patient—the wonderful life he had preserved, the fine job he had done—and Burnett seemed to have lost his professional compass.

Burnett tried to make his points clearly and without jargon of any kind. Jeffrey was alive, he said. Jeff's brain was functioning. Even if there were no further improvement in his condition, Jeffrey could think and talk and—Burnett used words that are apparently magical in the medical world—"interact with his environment."

I reminded Burnett that it was up to us, his parents, to decide whether that was enough. We could have argued about the meaning of the phrase. Single-cell creatures in a petri dish can interact with their environment. Worms and cockroaches do, as do baseball players, doctors, young girls in love, and cancer cells. But there was no need to argue about the meaning of the phrase; on this narrow question, Toby and I agreed with Burnett. Unless Jeff had suffered serious brain damage, yet undiscovered, Jeff would be able to interact with his environment in a sentient, meaningful, conscious, human way. We just disagreed over whether that was enough: whether Jeff should live because he was aware of his condition or die because he was.

"With all due respect—" Burnett began to say at one point. But I cut him off: "That's what a lawyer says just before he screws you," I said.

Burnett wanted us to know—he made it seem important that we know—that he had children of his own. He also didn't want us to give up hope for a recovery of some sort.

"There is still a window of opportunity," Burnett said. "Sometimes there is significant improvement in three months; sometimes improvement is detected in two years." On Saturday we had been told the window of opportunity was twenty-four hours. Now it was twenty-four months. Some window. Some marvelous, malleable window.

We talked about what "improvement" means to a high quadriplegic. How *much* improvement would there have to be for a C1-C2 to add significant value to his life? Could he improve enough to walk or use his hands? Could he improve enough to breathe? Neither doctor could tell us that the odds were in our favor.

Linda Snelling's face was relatively impassive, and she delivered her words softly, with a deliberate pace. Of the two doctors, she seemed at once more comfortable and more intense. To Burnett, our question about ending Jeffrey's life seemed unthinkable. To Snelling, our question was thinkable, *but that meant it required actual thought.* It was so much easier to say death was not an option. It was so much harder to admit that it was. Admitting that was just the start of the process. If death was an option, it had to be evaluated. Life and death had to be evaluated. If it was an option—as legitimate an option as any surgical procedure—then our consent and our choice for Jeffrey would have to be rational and informed.

At this point in the conversation, Dr. Snelling leaned forward in her chair. Her hands were together, her elbows were forward on her thighs, and she delivered her eyes that much nearer to us. I could not tell if she was trying to examine us more closely or trying to get us to pay more attention to what she had to say.

I told Dr. Snelling that if I had to make the decision at that moment—if it were the only chance I would get to make it—I would walk into Jeff's room and turn him off. I recognized, however, that no one had to execute the decision at that moment.

"The earlier you do it," Snelling said, "the easier it is to make the decision to 'let nature take its course.' But the earlier you make the decision, the less information you have. The decision is not reversible. You have to know enough to be sure."

We were not asking to do it now, I told her. But that was the outcome we expected if nothing changed.

And then we laid down what could have been taken for a challenge: we told them we needed to know, right now, whether there would be any opposition from the hospital. Was someone going to call in the lawyers? I asked.

In general, Dr. Snelling said, the hospital supported a family's decision. But there was a review process. Decisions like these were taken seriously and would be meaningfully reviewed. She would have to discuss the issue with others on the staff, including Dr. John Duncan, who was the chief of pediatric neurosurgery and therefore ultimately responsible for Jeff's care.

We told Dr. Snelling we would go through whatever review process was necessary. We told her to put the process in motion. Whatever we needed to do, we wanted to get done.

"When and if the time comes that we tell you the decision is final," I said, "we don't want to find out that there is another level of review, another hurdle to jump, that no one had mentioned yet."

In this meeting, as in subsequent meetings with the medical staff, Toby didn't say much. We knew what had to be said before the meeting started. As we talked, Toby concentrated on her personal, clear vision of Jeffrey. Her anguish was colored by recurrent memories of an earlier time when she had been brought into the company of invalids trapped in iron lungs. They lay still on their backs, with mirrors above their eyes to help them look backward into the small world that remained to them. Toby's memory of people in the iron lungs would blend into the fresher memory of Jeffrey in his bed down the hall, equally trapped without the metal envelope.

A long time after we had the meeting with Snelling and Burnett, I asked Toby what she had thought and felt, sitting next to her rabbi while we talked about ending Jeff's life. She said she had thought, briefly, that Les might believe she was a horrible person, but then she decided he would not. Over the years she had gotten to know his style of ministry. This thing Toby was putting him through —he could handle it. He wouldn't impose his judgment. She didn't need his judgment then. She needed his arm around her shoulders.

The discussion with Snelling and Burnett was methodical and substantively clear. I truly believe that any observer would have said that it was eloquent. We all spoke in complete sentences. There was no confusion. Each side spoke and listened carefully.

And yet I remember that much of the time I was slouched low in the couch with my face turned to the ceiling, an arm across my face, and tears boiling out of my eyes. I moaned once that I wished someone could convince me I was wrong because then I would get to keep my son. It was not the last time I would say that. But I think it was the first time, and I know I was quite a sorry sight when I said it. I think I apologized once or twice for my— let's put it kindly, shall we?—lack of composure. Sorry also for putting this burden on the hospital staff. How horrible we must have seemed to them.

Dr. Snelling tried to comfort me. She said that I was just trying to be an advocate for my son. She was correct, in an awful way. I was talking about my son. I was being an advocate as I did so. As a lawyer, I did that for a living. But out there where I learned my skills, I always asked my clients what they wanted before advocating the position to which they would be bound. In that hospital room, I was advocating a position that my son might never learn about.

"If we have to do this," I said, "Jeffrey will not be told. We don't want a crowd of people filing in to say good-bye, terrifying him."

I was being an advocate, all right. But out there in the real world, a defendant's lawyer doesn't argue for the death penalty.

Land Mines

Later I went home for the second time since the accident. I don't remember why I went—probably to get some clothes and such. It was an excruciating trip.

A long time ago I spent a year in Vietnam being more than fretful about land mines and booby traps. At home on Monday, after the accident, mines and traps were blowing up everywhere. All around me were memories, and all the memories were exploding. *Boom.*

As I rounded a curve in the road to my house, I saw the front yard. It was ripped apart for the landscaping project. I drove onto the new driveway and the new basketball court. As I rolled over the court, I remembered talking to Sarah about basketball: maybe she should learn; maybe if she practiced, she could even make the team. I had talked to her about the inexpressible joy of athletics at any level.

On July 3, when Sarah had agreed to go downtown and play with Jeff and me, I was surprised. Sarah started the game as a giggler. When she missed a shot or muffed a dribble, she giggled. Then she became frustrated because Jeff and I were controlling the ball. Finally, after a while, Sarah began to get serious. She never scored a point, but she started to make contact, to get physical. Twice she swatted the ball as I was trying to dribble by her; each time I complimented her boisterously.

It had been wonderful. In a week, I had thought, the new hoop will be in and we can do this every day. I was already planning to put in lights, to extend the season. As it turned out, that single sunny Friday afternoon was the first and last time that Sarah, Jeff, and I would ever play basketball together. On the following Monday, I drove over the driveway court knowing it would never happen again. *Boom.*

I stopped the car near our front door. The new brick walkways had just been installed. If Jeff came home, we would probably have to rip up some of the bricks or install a ramp over them. As I walked into the house, I waited for our dog, Kirby, to greet me. But now she was staying at a friend's house. Jeffrey wouldn't be able to walk her anymore, or even pat her head. *Boom.*

I entered the kitchen. We had just finished remodeling the first floor of the house. The kitchen was filled with light and was highlighted by blue-speckled granite countertops. Looking over the new granite, out through the new windows, I could see past the new deck into the backyard, which would be fenced in pretty soon for the dog—except that now I had to stop the landscaping project and maybe even sell the house and move. I called the landscaper and left a message.

Every object triggered a memory, and every memory was a land mine, and they all exploded. *Boom.*

When I threw some junk mail into the trash compactor, I thought, Jeffrey took out the garbage every Tuesday night. If he remembered to do it, we paid him three dollars. If he forgot to do it, he paid us three dollars. It had become a weekly ritual: Toby would remind him over and over, as each Tuesday evening turned to night, "Remember the garbage, Jeff; don't forget to take out the garbage." "Okay, all right," Jeff would say, with a teenager's confident exasperation, "don't worry, I'll do it." And sometimes he would remember, and sometimes he would forget. A weekly ritual about absolutely nothing, but still a part of the fabric of our lives. That was done for good. *Boom.*

There were eighteen messages on the answering machine. Most were from anguished friends and relatives. Two were from employers. Jeff's job applications had paid off. One wanted him to start work immediately. *Boom.*

Upstairs, as I walked into my bedroom, I saw a pile of shirts on the floor. Over a couple of weeks, I had been slowly sorting through shirts I had outgrown. Finally, Saturday morning, I pulled Jeff in and said, "Let's see which of these fit you and which you want." But none of them fit because his arms were much longer than mine. He was a big kid, taller and stronger than his father. On Saturday morning I realized I would have to give the shirts away because my big kid had outgrown me. He was taller, stronger, more handsome. But now things had changed. Only a few hours after he tried on the shirts, most of my big kid's body would be ruined. Gradually, its mass would shrivel. His arms would be thinner, weaker—but still longer than mine. In an instant I had become the healthy male of the family. In an instant my big kid's marvelous body had become dependent on the continued functioning of my own neglected carcass: the big belly, the ruptured lumbar disk, an assortment of other odd defects. I looked at the pile of my shirts and remembered how much of Jeff's wrists and arms had shown through them. I would have to get rid of that pile of shirts, I thought. *Boom.*

Out in the driveway, the car we had just restored, brought back to life, was waiting for its master. There was the snowboard rack he had installed on Friday dreaming of winter. And now I noticed the sunroof had been cracked open.

Before he left with us for the party on Saturday, Jeff had opened the sunroof to let out the hot air. He wanted the car to be cool when he returned that night so that he could finally take it for a ride. It would have been his first ride in his own car on a summer Saturday night. What was he thinking when he opened the sunroof Saturday afternoon? Did he have some place in particular to go that night? Was there someone he was going to meet? Or was he just going to follow the white lines down the road? The car had a good sound system, and music always felt different when you were burning petroleum. Maybe he would just start the car and drive. It would have been the first time in our lives that he could walk out the door and just *drive.*

I closed the sunroof. Jeff would never get to take that ride. *Boom.*

I needed to get something from Jeff's room—his CD player and disks. I went upstairs. Jeff would probably never get upstairs again. I found the CD player quickly and was about to leave but paused. Something was different about the room. I looked around. Jeff's desk was neat and so was his bureau. There were no piles of dirty laundry on the floor. His bed was made. I thought, That can't be. His bed is *never* made.

We had been battling for two years to get him to clean up his room, and he had never been willing to do it. And yet there it was: his room was clean, and his bed was made. It was the last time he would ever make a bed, but he had managed to make it, that one last time, just before being destroyed. *Boom.*

That was all I could take. I sat at the top of the stairs, elbows on knees and face in hands, and just cried. Because I knew what had happened on Saturday. I knew why Jeff's room was clean and his bed was made for the first time in years. He was saying thank you to Toby and me. In his own quiet, shy, teenager way, he was saying, Thanks for sticking with me.

After months of turmoil and worry, months of dark days, he had turned the slope of his life upward, and he was—finally—in balance, happy, and hopeful. He was a teenager beginning to have fun, beginning to realize his dreams. *Boom.*

It took me a long time to compose myself enough to drive back to the hospital. I came back into the family lounge—which was sprinkled with friends—quite weighed down. I told Toby, "You are not going to enjoy going home again."

•••••••••••••••••

I had been hoping against hope that the TV announcer had gotten it wrong . . . but when I heard your voice and learned it was our Jeffrey, my heart broke.—PAT CARLSON

•••••••••••••••••

The period between Saturday night and Monday night could not really be divided up into days. For us it was an irregular rush of time, in which things happened erratically, unpredictably, without any connection to the outside world. Night, day, evening, morning—it was all the same. We passed our time in the family lounge, in a smaller conference room (one couch, two chairs), and in Jeffrey's room, never knowing how long we would stay in any place or where we would go to next.

We had no solitude. Sometimes we were alone, but we were never private. I could lie on a couch and doze for an hour or more, then the phone would ring or a doctor —just starting a shift—would come in to see us. We would be in conversation with a group of friends. A nurse would tell us that Jeffrey was starting to wake up, and we would rush to see him. Sometimes we went to him too soon—Jeff was not alert yet—and retreated back to the lounge to pick up the conversation. Sometimes Jeff would be alert enough for us to stay with him. By the time we returned to the lounge an hour later, a new group of friends would be there to receive us. Conversations would be cut off in midsentence. As new batches of friends arrived, we would make our reports: the same questions, the same dismal answers, over and over again.

In the early days we were kept afloat by a sea of friendship, but we were also pulled under by our friends' own agony. A couple would arrive in the lounge for the first time, their eyes wide with compassion and fear. They would have heard the basics—a diving accident, almost a drowning, Jeff a quadriplegic—but then they would want to know: What did that mean? What did that mean for Jeffrey? And we would tell them. And as we told them, no matter how wrecked they seemed at the start, they fell into a deeper level of horror. And sometimes they took us down with them.

I am not a hugger. It seems, however, that this reluctance to hug is not shared by others, at least not in a crisis like ours. I got hugged by rabbis, lawyers, big people, little people, close friends, forgotten acquaintances, and strangers. And let's not fail to mention group hugs. They would form spontaneously. A couple would approach a wife. The two women would hug; then others would join. Then someone's arm would reach out—or was it a tentacle?—and I would be sucked in. Group hugs would form with us at the center. Group hugs would form among other people, without our participation. At times, the room seemed like a congregation of rugby scrums.

Dr. Duncan Arrives

To us, Dr. John Duncan was the boss. Our son was a patient in Duncan's domain. We had known about him since

Saturday or early Sunday, but because he was out of town, we didn't meet him until late on Monday.

He was younger than I had expected. He had an enviable mustache, a quiet air of confidence, and a manner of speaking that was direct but unhurried. He asked us to confirm what we knew of Jeffrey's condition. I repeated what Ken Burnett had said: it was as bad as it gets.

"In my opinion," Dr. Duncan told us, "the chance of your son achieving a substantial improvement in function is nil."

He started walking us through the near-term steps we would have to take. The information—medical procedures, treatment and rehabilitation options—was not new to us. I didn't wait long before breaking in.

"Because you have been away," I told him, "you may not have heard that we are considering termination of Jeffrey's life support."

Dr. Duncan didn't seem surprised. That meant he had been forewarned (likely) or that he was very hard to rattle (equally likely) or both.

We explained our thinking and described the earlier meeting with Ken Burnett and Linda Snelling. In a long conversation, we told Dr. Duncan who Jeffrey was and why we thought a life in quadriplegia could not be justified for him. We told Duncan, as we had told the others, that we were not asking to execute the decision now, but that we wanted to get any obstacles out of the way.

At some point in our conversation, I remember Dr. Snelling coming in. She said little. The meeting itself was inconclusive, in the sense that nothing was decided, nothing actually done. But the membership at the meeting was important. From the moment of Duncan's arrival, he and Snelling became our principal connections to the world of medicine. There were many others who treated Jeff and counseled us. But Duncan and Snelling were the two in whom we reposed the most confidence and through whom we expected decisions to be communicated.

This was, in a sense, a "get acquainted" meeting. Dr. Duncan met us and our intentions. We met him and reckoned the force he represented. If I had to guess, I'd say Toby and I left the meeting with more faith in Doctors Duncan and Snelling than they had in us. I didn't begrudge them their doubts. I had plenty of my own.

Taking Control

Later we met with Dr. Luks, the surgeon who had scheduled Jeffrey's tracheostomy for the next day. We sat in a small room, and he explained the procedure and its risks. Because Toby and I were the ones making decisions for our minor son, as a responsible physician Dr. Luks was seeking our informed consent for the operation.

We might not want the operation, we told him. We reminded him that we were considering whether to terminate Jeffrey's life support.

Dr. Luks was uncomfortable. Less than two days into the medical system, I had begun to realize that this would be the nearly universal response. These people—the doctors, the nurses, everyone—faced death every day. Yet they all seemed *startled* when someone from the outside world put death into the equation.

Imagine the look on an airline pilot's face if you stepped into his cockpit and told him, Thanks for your concern, but I'll take the controls from here. That's the look on a doctor's face when you offer to decide his patient's outcome.

It was only Monday, we were explaining our position to another doctor, and I got the feeling this would not be the last time. We described our son. We described our feelings for him. We described the reasons for our decision. And all the while, Dr. Luks viewed us with a kind of compassionate bewilderment. Each day this surgeon would dip his hands into warm blood and guts and living tissue, as if that were a natural thing for a person to do; yet this *conversation* seemed to strike him as unreal.

It was clear that Jeffrey needed the tracheostomy to continue his life, but we did not want to put him through that procedure if we were soon going to end his life. After a while we agreed that Jeffrey's tracheostomy would be taken off the next day's schedule, to be fit in later if needed.

Bedtime Stories

That evening, Jeffrey was awake. But he had also regressed. In his fear and despair, he seemed to have pulled himself into a smaller package.

We asked if he wanted us to read to him. He nodded yes. We struggled to find something suitable. I had an idea: *Goodnight Moon.* It was a book we had read to Jeffrey over and over, night after night, when he was a little child. When bedtime was the sweetest, most intimate moment we shared.

We carried the idea into the family lounge. There were a couple of boxes of books, and a friend or two helped us look through them for *Goodnight Moon*. Some of our friends tried to remember and write down the words to the book. After all, it had been *the* bedtime book of our entire parenting generation. Rabbi Gutterman insisted on going out to buy a copy of the book; he even had it gift wrapped. He said it was a privilege to do it.

And so, on Monday night, with our family crowded into a nest of wires and tubing, I read to Jeffrey the words that so long ago had helped to sustain him through his little-boyhood, while we tucked him into his dreams. I tried to read the book in a warm, clear voice, attentive to its rhythms.

As I read to him, I tried to remember those times when, while reading my son to sleep at night, I had wanted my son to wake up in the morning.

BACK IN THE family lounge, some friends were waiting. We talked. People had brought food, bags of it. I realized that I had not had a meal for two days. Someone told me I should eat.

"You have to eat," she said. "You have to keep up your strength."

I told her, "Do you think I'm going to squander all this anxiety on *gaining* weight?"

Since the accident, Toby had lost not only her appetite

but also her ability to eat. She would force herself to go to the cafeteria, put food on her tray, and sit at a table. But once the food was in her mouth, she could not chew or swallow. She started to drink flavored dietary supplements from cans.

The family lounge outside the Hasbro pediatric intensive care unit had taken on a character quite its own. At times it seemed like a wake; at other times, like a social club or a study group in medical school. One person would be telling a joke while someone else discussed the impact of steroids on the spinal column's myelin sheath. A wall-mounted TV was often on, which meant that at times our tragedy had a laugh track and commercial interruptions. People floated in and out. A basket with our name on it had been set upon a table near the door. People dropped cards and notes in the basket and surrounded it with food. We shared it with the families of other children who were patients at Hasbro.

So many conversations, and so many new people joined them. They cried with us, hugged us, did anything they could think of to make it better. They all had so much hope. They tried to give their hope to us, told us about articles they had read, disabled people they had known, and their own faith.

They would talk of the future, of Jeffrey's future. He still had a life. He could still live. He could still exist. They did not know that we were considering taking that life away. If they listened, they surely heard hints.

One woman said to me, "At least he can feel. At least he can still feel things."

I replied, "If you stick your hand into a fire, you will feel it."

AS THE NIGHT passed and our friends receded back to their other world, Toby and I were left alone finally, to think and then to sleep. I sat for a while with the lights off. I tried to take stock of our lives to that point. I tried to imagine the future without Jeff.

I had told Toby early in the crisis that this would not end well. By Monday night I realized that the decision to kill Jeff or to help him live wouldn't ever end, not ever. It would reverberate in my mind as long as I had a living mind to let it. I would always question whatever decision I made; I would always have doubts. Even if others let the issue rest after a while, I never would.

At some point the decision would have to be made. Life or death. As simple as that. At what point we had to make the decision, I didn't know. There was no deadline. Neat concept, "deadline." We had none. We had a kid languishing in anguish, with a bleak future before us. Whatever choice we made would be the wrong one.

By Monday night, July 6, I had begun to conceptualize what life would be like after it was over. I wrote a note to myself:

We rescued him from death and then we rescued him from life. We will never be sure that either rescue was best for him.

Looking back, I can see now how fixed my determination was just two days after the accident. While I was constantly evaluating the decision—lifting myself to a higher and more rigorous level of analysis—the operating premise was that Jeffrey would die. My last thoughts Monday night were not whether to let him go, but how to explain it to myself and others after it was done.

Looking back, I can also see how foolish was the attempt by anyone—myself included—to soften by language the stern stuff of our intentions. Poets might "rescue" people from life. Poets have the luxury of inventing the myths they write about. But when fathers shut off life support, they don't "rescue" their sons from life. They "kill" their sons. Before I went to sleep on Monday night, I came back to reality.

This is the last night, I thought, that my son may be alive. When I wake in the morning, I may kill him.

It took me a long time to let that thought sink in. When I finally lay down on the couch, I went to sleep immediately.

....

I just keep trying to imagine what this must be like for
you . . .wishing it would all just go away and
you could resume life as before . . . please know that
I—and a zillion other folks—are here—praying,
worrying, hoping, thinking about you, and sending
you that collective energy, to add to your own,
to get through this.—MARGE LEDERER

....

Tuesday, July 7

....

WHEN I AWOKE ON TUESDAY MORNING, EVEN BEFORE
my eyes opened, I asked myself, Is this the morning of the
day that I kill my son? I sat up, then sat cross-legged on the
couch for a long time. A very long time.

When Toby came in, I said to her, "I have a problem. I
still think we may have to pull Jeff's life support. I still believe that may be the right decision. But I am bothered because it seems too easy to make. I can't figure out why I
can make this decision without doing any research at all.

"I would do more research if I were buying a toaster," I
said.

"What do you think we should do?" Toby asked.

"I think I want to be professional about it. I want to treat Jeffrey as if he were my client. I want to take some time, visit some of the rehab hospitals, and do what I would do if Jeffrey were my client and he were asking for my professional advice."

Toby was relieved. The pressure was off, at least for a little while. It made so much sense to hold back. It felt so good to know it would not happen that day. Maybe the next day, but not now.

When Dr. Snelling arrived, I told her the same thing: I'd spend more time researching the purchase of a toaster. I had to be professional and treat my son like a client. She approved. But then I told her: "Don't expect me to change my mind. Don't expect the decision to be different."

We decided to put Jeff back on the schedule for the tracheostomy the next morning. That way, regardless of where the decision ended up going, our time with Jeffrey would be better: more comfortable for him and, with the tubes out of his mouth, easier for us to communicate.

Mirror Images

When we next saw Jeffrey, he was unusually alert and somber. He told us he wanted a mirror so that he could see himself. Toby had a small, rectangular mirror in a plastic case. I held it above Jeffrey and slowly turned it up and down, side to side.

When he saw himself, and all the machinery, and all the wires and tubes that connected to his numb body, his face showed shock—but not as much as I expected.

"This sucks," he mouthed.

I used the mirror to point out and describe the major pieces of equipment, especially his ventilator. I explained that a portable model would fit on his wheelchair so that he could move around.

We tried to talk a bit, but Jeffrey was almost disabled by discomfort. He begged us to elevate his head, raise him up. He had been level on his back for almost three days. He pleaded with us to let him sit up, to see level for just a little while. I told him I couldn't do it.

"I've ruined my life," he said.

He told me he wanted it all to be over. What did he want to be over? The process, he said. "What process?" I asked. Whatever it is, he replied, just get it done. I told him the process would lead him to a wheelchair. Just do it, he said. Get it over.

He said he wanted drugs. He wanted to be drugged to sleep. He said he wanted to be drugged until the process was done. He said he didn't want to wake up to talk to us.

Too Tough for the Professionals

With the help of Paul Taraborelli, our Hasbro social worker, Toby and I arranged a visit that afternoon at a rehabilitation hospital in Braintree, Massachusetts—the facility that the doctors had mentioned in our meeting on Monday.

We drove to Braintree, mostly in silence. We parked the car, asked to see our contact, and waited. We were early. I spent time looking at some upbeat photos mounted on the walls; then I watched the people passing by: residents, visitors, and staff. Then I began organizing my thoughts about Jeff's entry into this next stage of the system:

- When Jeff is thirty, I will be sixty-five.
- When Jeff is forty, I will be seventy-five. The likelihood that Jeff will be living at home with his parents will have dwindled.
- At some point, when Jeff is still much younger than I am now, he will be at once helpless and on his own. At some point reasonably early in his life, he will be locked in the care of people for whom—and I try to think of them kindly—Jeffrey will be part of their job.

As I sat in the waiting area at Braintree, I wrote in my notebook, "There is no way out of this without someone dying."

Even if Jeffrey's consent turned out to be necessary for the ending of his life support, I was sure I could get it. If the plain horror of his situation did not convince him, I might have to strike a bargain. To convince him that he shouldn't be afraid of death, I would promise to die along with him. He would not wake up, and I would kill myself soon after. That would do it.

I thought, How do you kill your son and go on living? How do you kill your son, then see a movie, eat a meal, or play a game of tennis? That was unimaginable. If chance killed him—well, there would be mourning and a lifelong sense of loss . . . but someday there would be healing, and there would be movies and meals and tennis.

But if I kill my son, do I expect that to heal? I do not. So my thinking started to settle on a more complete form of closure. When he goes, we both go. Interesting thought. Pretty fair, too, when I thought about it some more. Pretty damn equitable.

Unbelievably, I was having these thoughts and taking notes on them, as I sat beside my wife, about to interview a lady about Jeffrey's placement in her hospital, where the goal was *to teach Jeff how to live.*

This is nonsense, I thought as I finally caught myself. My plans and my goals were conflicting and nonsensical, and possibly delusional. You don't plan your son's death in the place where they teach optimism. Okay, so you're under pressure and can be forgiven a few eccentricities. But when the *Titanic* hits the iceberg, you go down with the ship or jump off and swim; you *don't* ask to book a room.

As I settled back into sanity, I gave myself an out. After all, what sane choice did I have that was satisfying? What difference did it make if I became inconsistent, haphazard, unfocused, or bizarre? There is no good solution to this situation, I reminded myself. No matter what, this thing doesn't end well.

When our contact at Braintree finally took us into her office, she apologized. Braintree did not take ventilator-dependent patients in Jeff's condition. She quickly arranged a visit to a facility in Worcester, and we drove there right away.

On the way to Worcester, Toby was furious. Her lid blew off. She was angry at the people at Hasbro for suggesting the Braintree hospital. Why did they waste our time? She was angry at Jeffrey. Why had he not been more careful? She was angry at the pool. Why had there been no depth markers? She was angry at the Goldsteins. Why? Having a pool? Having an unsafe pool? Having a party?

When cultivated, anger blossoms. The accident should not have happened. It must have been preventable. It must have been someone's fault. I tried to get Toby to stop.

"You can't do this," I said. "You can't let yourself get worked up about it. It isn't productive." That just got her more angry, this time at me. She thought I had written her off.

"You told me to give up my anger," she reminded me later, when we talked about that awful trip. If I had said that, it was a horrible piece of advice. The trick wasn't giving up the anger she had; the trick was not getting angry in the first place.

At any rate, having been sent packing from Braintree, we drove to Worcester in a foul mood. When we reached the rehab hospital in Worcester, it took only a few minutes to realize they were not set up for Jeffrey either. Although sympathetic, they had nothing of value to offer us.

We drove back to Providence in a bottomless funk. Yes, there were rehab hospitals where paralyzed people are prepared to meet their new worlds. We had seen two. Neither could handle Jeff. He was out of their league, too hard a case, too paralyzed. They did not have the right equipment, they did not have the right program, they did not have the right staff to care for Jeff for even a few weeks before he came home to his parents, the amateurs, who had no tools or experience to offer but couldn't refuse.

Back at Hasbro, we were happy to learn that Jeff's doctors had changed his medication orders. Jeff's schedule had been hectic, and his sleeping sporadic. The doctors now wanted him to have a more normal day/night schedule. So, starting Tuesday night, Jeff would be given a continuous intravenous dosage that would insure that he would sleep the whole night through. This would give Toby and me a chance to rest as well, and we were grateful to get it. We checked with the staff, and being assured that we would have the time, Toby and I decided to spend our first night together at home in East Greenwich.

In the middle of the night, we were roused by a phone call. The hospital's night staff had not put Jeff on the schedule we had been promised. They had followed the old orders, not the new ones. They had eased up on his meds, reduced his dosage; and Jeff had awakened in a panic. He was calling for us. He was terrified. He was sure that we had abandoned him.

I know we cannot fathom the unspeakable shock and grief that has befallen your Jeffrey and, indeed, all of you . . . Jeffrey is otherwise healthy and strong. That, coupled with the accelerating pace of technology, can be a source of hope. Time and medical innovation are clearly on his side.—NIKKI PIKUS

Wednesday, July 8

EARLY WEDNESDAY MORNING, WE VISITED THE REHA-bilitation Hospital of Rhode Island, in North Smithfield. They were sympathetic and informative. They were willing to help; in fact they were eager to help. But they were not spinal specialists. They were certainly not specialists in paralysis at the very highest level, with complete ventilator dependency.

We talked a lot about where Jeff might go after leaving their hospital. He could go home, or he could go . . . well, *elsewhere.*

Toby had been a state social worker and was now a discharge planner for a psychiatric hospital. She knew what the staff in North Smithfield now confirmed. There was nothing very good very close. In the region, there were a couple of long-term hospitals taking vent quads like Jeffrey, and a couple of nursing homes. But nothing would deliver an experience for Jeffrey even remotely like living at home.

And our North Smithfield hosts cautioned us about the toll we would pay for having him at home. The question was not whether we wanted to care for him. The question was whether we would be able to do it and for how long.

Jeffrey would have to be hoisted out of bed each morning and hoisted back each night in some kind of mechanical lift. He would have to be turned in bed frequently, to avoid pressure sores. He was on a vent machine, which made every process tougher and more hazardous.

Someone would have to help him move his bowels, probably in bed, and someone would have to look after the catheters for his urine. He would have to be dressed and undressed. He would have to be fed and shaved, and his teeth brushed. Mucus would have to be suctioned from his lungs, using a vacuum machine and tubes pushed down into his trachea.

Hired help—nurses or home care attendants—would do some of it. But some combination of people would have to do *all* of it twenty-four hours a day, every day, for the rest of Jeff's life. There would be no holidays.

These people wanted Jeff to have the best life possible but were cautious about bringing him home. Toby and I needed to work, to make a living, they reminded us. We would need physical strength and stamina to care for him. We could not do it forever. At some point he would leave us, or older and less capable ourselves, we would leave him.

Most people in Jeffrey's condition did go home, they told us. They were less certain about how long those people stayed at home.

Evidence

On the way back to Hasbro, Toby and I talked about our options.

Toby doubted we could pull it off. We had no live-in friends or family who could provide the kind of help Jeff needed. Toby was most concerned about where Jeff could go when he could no longer live with us.

"He's beyond what a nursing home could take care of," she said. She couldn't bear to think of him in larger, colder institutions such as chronic care hospitals. She couldn't bear to think of him on a shelf, in a warehouse, kept alive and out of sight.

I was more interested in second-guessing my assumptions. I could not honestly say it was hopeless. At least for a while, Jeff could be a viable member of the family. We could find a way to pay for his medical equipment. If insurance didn't cover it, we could cash in his assets and my retirement fund. Moving to another house would not be a problem. Neither would my job. If I had to, I would wind up my firm and open up a smaller practice at home.

The fact was that we knew it could be done. We knew we could get Jeff into rehab, and we knew he could come out in a wheelchair, able to move on his own. We knew the machines could keep him breathing. We knew that with help we could take care of his cleaning, getting him in and out of bed, and all of that.

Everything they have been telling us was true, I said to Toby. We could do all of that, at least for a while.

But, I told Toby, I hadn't changed my mind. I still thought Jeff would be better off not going through all that. After a period of silence, I said that the research we were doing would simply confirm that the life of quadriplegics could be saved and preserved, just as the doctors told us it could.

"At the end," I said, "I'll be left with all of the evidence on one side, and only my opinion on the other."

Don't Rush

Whenever Toby and I initiated discussion of Jeff's death with his doctors, we made them take us seriously because of the force of our conviction. We didn't necessarily convince them that our decision would be correct, just that serious people would be making it.

The one argument we found hard to oppose was this: We shouldn't rush. We shouldn't decide yet. We should take time. And believe it or not, in the short space of a few days, in the midst of all the turmoil, we found some time to get smarter.

I read two books by recent quadriplegics: Christopher Reeve, the famous actor who had broken his neck when his horse refused a jump, and Travis Roy, a young hockey player whose injury came eleven seconds into his first college game. I read an introductory treatise on spinal cord injuries. And our friends were feeding us research from the Internet and other sources.

No one at the hospital agreed that terminating Jeff's life support was the right decision to make. Some told us they thought it was the wrong decision; some told us they would make a different decision themselves; and some told us it ought to be Jeff's decision, not ours.

I remember in particular a meeting with Dr. Stuart Bodner, Jeff's pediatrician. I reminded Dr. Bodner that as the parents of a minor patient, Toby and I had the right to make all of the decisions concerning Jeff's medical care or its termination.

But that was not fair, Dr. Bodner told me with passion. It was not fair to Jeff. It was his life. In a few weeks, he would be eighteen years old. It would be his decision then. It ought to be his decision now. He had to be asked. He had to make the decision himself.

On that issue, I had already been tested. Now I tested Dr. Bodner.

"Would you say the same thing," I asked him, "if Jeffrey said he wanted to die, and Toby and I said we wanted him to live?"

Dr. Bodner had nothing to say in response. Because we both knew that in his mind, and in the minds of many others, the authority to make the decision shifted according to the outcome chosen. The authority shifted to whoever chose life instead of death. If Jeff chose life, it was his choice absolutely. If Jeff chose death, it was only because of the drugs, or the shock, or the depression, or the tender years, and we should refuse him.

The fact was, I told Dr. Bodner, the law gave us the right to make these decisions. Somebody had to have the right —and the obligation—and the law said it was his parents. It was us. And that was just the way it was. And we would make the decision. And that would be that.

And at least for the moment, I would ignore the fact that Jeff had already told me more than once that he wanted to die. I was not ready to let Jeff decide. I was not ready to share the blame.

Testing Our Resolve

Later that afternoon, we had two meetings with doctors. The first, a brief one, was with Susan Pakula, who had been Jeffrey's pediatrician when he was a little boy. Sue stayed for the second, larger meeting of the day. We were joined by Doctors Duncan and Snelling, Dr. Gregory Fritz (Jeff's staff psychiatrist) and a young woman who was a medical student at Dartmouth.

Although we discussed Jeffrey's condition and his care, clearly the point of the meeting was to test our resolve to end his life. We gave them our report.

- Jeff could survive for years.
- Current technology would permit him to move by his own command, once he was placed in a powered chair.
- He could breathe using portable machines, and if some upper-body muscle control returned, he might be weaned to breathe on his own for a part of each day.

- He could speak on his own for much of the day, and if that didn't work, he could use an artificial larynx to generate speaking sounds.

"We are assuming," I said, "that Jeffrey maxes out every range of options open to us. On every issue, we assume the best of all possible results.

"And yet," I concluded, "we have not changed our minds. We still think that Jeffrey should not leave this hospital alive."

The doctors asked us to tell them about our own experiences with death. I told them about Vietnam and auto accidents I had seen or covered as a reporter. Toby confessed that she was terrified of dying.

One of the doctors asked me what Jeffrey would want for himself. I told him, "You should act on the assumption that Jeffrey is a teenage boy who desperately wants to live. You can assume that is the answer he would give if you put the question to him now."

But we didn't want the question put to him. If the decision was made to terminate his life support, we didn't want him waiting in terror for it to happen. If we could arrange it, at some point when Jeff went to sleep, he would not wake up again.

For the first time, I think, the doctors in the group could sense that the decision was becoming—there is no other word for it—*real*.

One of them mentioned that they tried to keep medical decisions confidential, but what we were planning would almost certainly get out.

"A lot of people are going to be critical of us," Toby said. "People are not going to understand how we could make a decision like this for a child who was alive and alert."

Toby expressed her concern about the effect it would have on other members of our family, especially fourteen-year-old Sarah. Imagine how Sarah would feel if she learned that her parents were capable of killing their children. Imagine what our friends would say, not only everyone who had been sharing in our grief but the wider community that had been staggered by the news as well.

If Jeffrey were allowed to die, Toby said, she didn't want to discuss the decision with anyone. It was our decision. It was private. It should stay that way.

We broke ranks.

"We shouldn't run away from the decision," I said. "I expect to tell people exactly what we did. If there is to be an uproar in the community, better that it be over a fact plainly stated than a secret cowardly kept.

"Besides," I said, "the community ought to know that decisions like these are being made." And, I might have said, that people—anybody—can some day find themselves having to make them.

Looking back on the discussion, it is amazing that we never resolved this dispute between Toby and me on the issue of privacy. She said her piece, I said mine, and we moved on as if the rift had closed. Maybe we both knew, intuitively, that it was far more important to make the right decision than to worry about whether or how it would be revealed.

"I don't want to kill my son," I said. "But I think we have to. I am convinced that in moments of clarity, if he knew what we know, if he understood his situation, he would make the same decision. I know it.

"And I hate being so certain of it. I wish I had some doubt. I wish I had the same kind of hope that others have. But I don't. I know what we have to do. I know it. And so we will make the decision. And we may have to kill our son.

"And I know that for the rest of my life I will have to live with it. Some people will hate us for it. I can name some right now. But I can take the weight. I can take the heat. And I know for the rest of my life I will have doubts that we made the right decision.

"But that is the price we have to pay for the *privilege* of making the decision. And the price is cheap," I said, "because by paying it, we get to make the decision for our son."

Dr. Duncan cut in, finally.

"We don't kill our patients here," he said, "and you aren't going to kill your son."

"I use that word," I told him, "because it is the worst word I can use. It makes the decision as hard as possible. The harder it is to make the decision, the more sure I am that it will be right if we make it."

"As a family," Duncan said, "you have the right to decide what level of care is right for your son. You may decide that his ventilator support is a medical service that ought to be removed, and if it is removed, Jeffrey may not be able to survive on his own. But we don't kill our patients here."

"Dr. Duncan," I said, "if the vent is removed and Jeffrey breathes on his own, I will be the first to tell you to hook it up again and let's see what else we were wrong about."

We asked them once more about the process. There had already been several meetings with several doctors. What was left to be done? What other hurdles were there?

At least one remained, they said: the hospital's ethics committee ought to be consulted. Would we mind talking to them or at least to its chair?

We would talk to as many people as they wanted us to, we told them. We just wanted to know, at some point soon, that the hurdles had all been jumped. In the meantime, we would talk to anybody.

"After all," I said, "I can't lose. If someone convinces me I'm wrong, I get to keep my son."

....

I continue to say a prayer daily for your son. Although I do not know him, he is always in my thoughts.

—JANET HARRINGTON

....

Losses, Deficits, and Voids

Each aspect of Jeffrey's life that was lost or diminished required some kind of change to occur in Jeff. Each loss of function also represented a loss of personality. For example, consider the loss of his legs.

- He lost the ability to walk upstairs to his bedroom.
- He lost the ability to run and jump in a pickup basketball game.
- He lost the ability to compete for a spot on the high school basketball team.
- He lost the ability to walk down the aisle at his wedding.
- He lost the ability to carry the coffin of a friend or relative.
- He lost the ability to tangle his legs with those of a lover.
- He lost the ability to sit back on the couch, legs crossed on the glass-topped table, bowl of popcorn in his lap, watching TV.

I would never be able to evaluate Jeff's losses with any degree of precision. Jeff played basketball. So did Michael Jordan. If both Jeff and Michael Jordan lost their legs, I didn't know which man would suffer more. I did know that the loss of his legs would be, to my particular son, a terrible, terrible thing.

Jeffrey was a modest boy. For example, since puberty, I had not seen his penis. If he was too long in the shower and I knocked on the bathroom door, he would shout, *"Don't come in!"* with real force. On the few occasions when I stepped into his bedroom and he was naked, he would spin around, using his T-shirt or just his cupped hands to shield his private parts.

I knew there were many times when he exposed himself to the eyes of strangers: showers at the high school gym or the pool club, for example. But when he could be modest, he chose to be modest.

That was the old Jeff. In his new life, Jeff would have to surrender his modesty. He would have to get used to people seeing his penis. Nurses, hired home care attendants, perhaps in time even his younger sister. Over the years, dozens of people, maybe hundreds, never by his choice. Because he had to, he would suppress his modesty.

The old, modest Jeffrey was gone. The new, exposed Jeffrey had taken his place. The new Jeffrey would have to change psychologically—in mood, in perception of his intimate self—if he were to survive without at least that little bit of added torment.

Change or torment: that would be the essence of his adaptation. The less he changed, the greater would be his torment.

Given all his other losses, how could I be concerned with Jeffrey's loss of modesty? I thought about that. What was modesty compared to walking? What was modesty compared to breathing or using his hands?

I knew all I needed to know: Jeffrey's modesty lived inside Jeffrey above the C1-C2 level. Jeffrey's modesty was an incidental casualty of the other losses. Jeffrey was suffering losses of personality. Modesty was only one. How many others there were, I didn't know. Even in his mind, above the broken neck, Jeffrey was taking losses. The stuff that made Jeffrey our singular, unique, familiar son . . . that stuff was leaking.

Two Whom Chance Ignored

In the afternoon our visitors included Ed Maggiacomo, one of the founders of a law firm in which I had worked for fifteen years. I had left in 1991 to start a small firm of my own, in large part because I wanted to run a business and become a "grown-up" like Ed.

About fifteen years ago, one of Ed's four children—a teenage boy like Jeff—was skiing, zoomed off the edge of the trail, and struck a tree. Michael lay in a coma for a short time before his death. I was an usher at Michael's funeral. Now here Ed and I were, years later, hugging, as my own son lay paralyzed and fighting for life, another young victim of having too much fun.

Ed told me a story—actually a set of interrelated stories.

"When my son died," he said, "it was my job to be the leader of the family. The wake, the funeral, making arrangements, dealing with friends and relatives, expressing our feelings in a public way. It was hard. But I had to be strong for the family. I kept my emotions under control, and I did what I had to do.

"Then," he said, "about six months later, another close relative died, unexpectedly and tragically. The loss was painful, but again I found myself in a position where I had to be strong for the family. I had to keep my emotions under control.

"About six months after that," Ed said, "a friend of mine died. And I fell to pieces. I was disabled by grief.

People asked me why my friend's death had done that to me, when the other two had not. And I told them: this time I didn't have to be strong. It was not my job this time."

AFTER ED LEFT, an earlier memory floated back to me.

A bunch of people from our law firm spent a weekend at the Maggiacomo winter house near Loon Mountain in New Hampshire. After a really fine meal and more than enough to drink, Ed and I noticed that it was a perfect night for a ride on his snowmobile. The two of us saddled up and set off for the woods. It was utterly dark except for the snowmobile's headlight. We roared along the bank of a creek. The bite of the cold air, the dancing headlight playing off the trees, the branches snapping at us, and the sound of the engine all added to the unconstrained, roller coaster thrill of the ride. Eventually, we took a bump too sloppily, and we were tossed into the air. We came down on our backs, smashed together, half in the frigid brook, with the snowmobile on top of us.

We found ourselves in a tight place, not quite crushed and not quite drowned, laughing our silly heads off. What fun. We managed to get up and go home. At the time, that didn't seem like such a big deal. That day, chance was busy elsewhere.

We had done everything wrong. Everything. There was not a part of it that was prudent, responsible, or mature. If any two people deserved broken necks or fatal concussions, Ed and I did that night. But we didn't get them.

I'm sorry, Michael. I'm sorry, Jeff.

When I think of it, I almost cry. But I still almost laugh as well.

His Voice Returns

We got a summons from a nurse who had a surprise: she said Jeffrey wanted to see us. She said Jeff was asking a lot of questions. She said Jeff was *talking*.

And he was. The new tracheostomy tube had an inflatable cuff, like a hollow rubber doughnut, which acted as a seal. When the cuff was deflated, some of the air would leak past the cuff and exit over Jeff's vocal cords. Jeff could steal the breath he needed to speak.

Now that he could speak, the pent-up feelings of his last few days came out. There was no glad in Jeffrey.

"My life is over," he told us. "I ruined my life."

He told us he wanted to take it over. Like a do-over? I asked. Yes, he said. What did he want to take over? I asked. "Everything," he said.

He told us to make it stop. Stop what? I asked. "Everything," he said.

I leaned close to him. "You told me to do that two days ago," I said to him. "If I had done what you said then, we would not be talking to each other now. We would not have had these two days together. Do you understand?"

He nodded.

"Jeffrey, I know it's hard," I told him. "Things will be different. Your life will be different. But you will still be you. There are some things you won't be able to do anymore. There are some things you will have to do in different ways. You used to walk from the living room to the kitchen on your legs. Now you will drive from the living room to the kitchen in your chair. But either way, you will get from the living room to the kitchen.

"They saved the best parts of you," I said again, as I had before. "They saved your head and your heart." As I spoke, I touched his forehead, then his chest.

Artificial Means

Later we were visited by Rabbi Michael Cahana, Les Gutterman's colleague at Temple Beth-El. For a few minutes we had a conversation that meandered around, unfocused. Finally, we invited him to talk about Jeff's life support: What did Judaism have to say about removing it?

Under traditional Jewish law, he said, life was considered a gift from God. Because of that, life was absolutely valuable and had to be preserved by any means available. A Jew would not be permitted to withhold from a dying man the means to extend his life.

Obviously, the rabbi said, the traditional view had been developed long ago, when life expectancies were shorter and there were few useful tools available to ward off death.

However, with the advent of advanced medical technologies, some Jews had begun to fashion a distinction between "natural" and "unnatural" methods of prolonging life. Under that view, food and water were "natural" and could not be withdrawn even from a person in a vegetative state. But a ventilator—an electrical device with plastic tubes—would be considered "unnatural" and could be withdrawn.

That didn't seem correct, I said. It didn't seem reasonable that the choice should be determined in that way. After all, if the basis for the decision was whether the *device* was natural or unnatural, could a believing Jew withdraw mechanical ventilation from a patient who could walk and talk and was otherwise healthy?

At this point our conversation was interrupted, as so many others had been during those first few days. Toby and I were pulled out of the room and back into the system. I never had a chance to renew the talk with Rabbi Cahana, much as I wanted to. I was selfish: I enjoyed the intellectual stimulation of such a discussion. It was—I'm not sorry to say it—an entertaining diversion.

I recognize now—and did then—that I had Rabbi Cahana at a disadvantage. While he would have been informative had the conversation continued, I also know he would have been kind. It is not likely that he would have said anything so plainly, or with such conviction, that he would add to our burden. For me, our conversation was in part a diversion from the harsh reality of life that day, but for him the conversation was part of his ministry.

Had we continued the conversation, there is one point in particular that I would have made to him: Jews are absolutely wrong that life is a gift from God. It is, at most, a loan. The loan is always called, and it is always, always repaid.

The Ethics Committee

We were told that the hospital's full ethics committee had decided to review our case. This was to be that "final hurdle" that we had sought.

Shortly before the ethics committee meeting was to convene, Dr. Snelling came to see us. The group attending the meeting, she said, would be a bit larger than expected. Some of the doctors and nurses caring for Jeffrey had asked to participate, even though they were not members of the committee. Did we have any objection? Dr. Snelling asked.

No, I said, I didn't mind. We would be happy to have them. But, I said, I did have one concern. Without saying it, I wondered if the meeting was being stacked by people who were determined to take a stand against us. I told Doctor Snelling that I hoped people were not nominating themselves to attend because they had some personal agenda to enforce. Dr. Snelling assured me that was not the intent of those who had asked to participate.

We were led to a conference room. About twenty people were arranged around a table and against the walls. Dr. Ed Forman introduced himself as the chair of the committee. The others at the meeting told us their names and specialties. Then Dr. Forman turned the meeting over to us.

I asked Toby to speak first, but she declined. She told me later that she didn't know if she would have been coherent. She wasn't organized in a rhetorical sense. The meeting was not about love or anguish. It was about persuasion.

If hell had an entrance exam, this meeting would have been the oral portion.

When Toby declined to speak, I began.

"You are all here," I said, "because you have heard that Toby and I are considering removing life support from our son, Jeffrey. You want to know whether we have given that decision enough thought, and whether we are well informed about the issues that might affect our decision. So let me give you a short history and tell you how we got here.

"Jeffrey was injured last Saturday. He is a C1-C2 quadriplegic, with no use of anything below his neck. We have been told that the injury is complete, in the sense that there is no residual response below the level of the injury. We have been advised that there is no reasonable expectation that he will improve substantially unless there is some breakthrough—unexpected at this point—in the treatment of spinal cord injuries. He is breathing by ventilator, and we have been advised that this will continue for the rest of his life.

"Over the past few days, in addition to talking to your staff, we have tried to learn things on our own.

"Our research is conclusive on at least these points: If Jeffrey spends an insignificantly short time—whether it's six weeks or six months, it's insignificantly short—at a rehab hospital, he will leave able to speak and to move in a wheelchair. He will need round-the-clock care because of his breathing, but with help he will be able to go to high school and maybe to college.

"Everything you have told us about Jeffrey's potential is

true. When we say that we believe you all, you can be sure that our belief is real and that it is based on information and not just our assumptions.

"When I talk to Jeffrey," I said to the group, "I divide his situation into three parts.

"The first part is his loss. I am very frank with him about the major losses of his legs and arms and hands. He knows he should not expect to walk again, or use his arms and hands again, or ever regain feeling in his lower body. I don't lie to my son, and when he asks me whether he will recover, I tell him what his doctors have told me.

"There is a second part, which I do not discuss with Jeffrey at all. I do not tell him about the medical complications resulting from the loss of his trunk and limbs. I have not told him about urine backing up into his kidneys; or about bowel programs; or about skin integrity, breakdown, and bedsores; or about opportunistic infections, which will come anytime and whose symptoms he won't even feel.

"The third part is his potential, what he can do with the parts of him that still work. And here I tell him that the parts remaining can do marvelous things. I tell him that the possibilities are almost limitless. I am a computer nut, and Jeffrey also knows computers. I tell him that with the right switches he can do almost anything. I touch his eyebrows, his nose, his lips, and tell him those are all switching mechanisms. He can move around; he can control a TV or stereo; he can surf the Net; and if he wants to, he can correspond by E-mail with some kid in China. I tell him there are gizmos out there we haven't even heard of yet, and if we need one they don't make, we'll make it ourselves.

"The point is to push him, always, to see the best and the brightest of all possible future scenarios, without lying to him."

I don't remember pausing during this little speech. As I spoke, I would look from face to face. So far, no one in the group seemed anxious to break in.

At the time, Toby was thinking, These are the people with the power to decide whether our decision will be allowed. They could block it. They could make a mess. They could bring us to court and to the press. They could deliver our decision, and therefore our son, to the wider world, with its egos and agendas and its vicious, soul-destroying celebrity.

Toby didn't know if we were unique or typical. Did parents often terminate the lives of their quadriplegic children? Had these people dealt with this situation before? Were we just going through the standard review, which preceded the standard method of termination? Or was this the process by which civilized providers of medical care smoke out monsters?

"My wife and I have to consider not just what will happen to Jeffrey this week or this year," I continued, "but also what will happen to him in the future. Everyone wants us to be hopeful, but we have to be realistic. On the subject of technology—how computers and other things will let Jeffrey use what he has left—we are extremely optimistic.

"But what about a *cure*? What are the chances that someone is going to find a cure for this type of injury? So far, I haven't heard of anything.

"From what I can see, most of the progress has been made in keeping paralyzed people alive. Twenty years ago," I said, "a person with an injury this high and this severe probably would have died; now he lives. But let me ask all of you: Is there anyone willing to say that twenty years from now a person with this injury will walk?"

I looked around the room. No hands were raised. A couple of people were shaking their heads silently.

"And let me ask you this: If they find a cure for this disease in ten years, is it likely that the cure will help someone who has already been in a chair for ten years?"

Again, no volunteers to tell me I was wrong.

"I haven't spoken to Jeffrey about his life expectancy," I said. "But I have had some experience in this area. I know what the outlook is for injured people who end up in wheelchairs. Is there anybody here who thinks he is more likely than not to live past his fifties?"

No one responded.

"Now let's talk about his body, the part of him he cannot use. For the rest of his life, we will all be fighting a losing battle against deterioration. Take Christopher Reeve: with all his money, with all his contacts and influence, Christopher Reeve got bedsores that ate to his bones.

"Tell me," I asked. "Has there been any significant leap in the treatment of bedsores in the last one hundred years?" No one spoke.

"I know everyone here wants the best for Jeffrey and for

our family," I continued. "And I know there are some people who do well after injuries like this. Everyone talks about Christopher Reeve and Travis Roy because they wrote these hopeful books and they are doing so well.

"Christopher Reeve is an extremely brave person, and the way he has reacted to his injury is remarkable. But when he was hurt, he was forty-two years old. He was rich and famous and had wonderful friends who rallied around him. And he also had a wife who stuck with him, and three children. And he had two gorgeous pieces of land, on which he had two homes, and while sitting on his deck he could look out over his land and the buildings in which he used to store his sailplanes and horses.

"Jeffrey," I said, "is not Christopher Reeve. He is seventeen years old. He doesn't have a wife or even a girlfriend. He doesn't have a career. No one is going to ask Jeffrey to direct a movie or fly him to the West Coast to give speeches. Jeff doesn't have the support Chris Reeve has, and he doesn't have the memories.

"And Travis Roy: he is also a very brave guy. But when he was unlucky enough to be paralyzed while playing in a hockey game, he was lucky enough to have the moment of his injury videotaped and broadcast on network TV. People all over the country were sending money to him. He had a girlfriend who stuck with him. He was famous; people were asking him to give lectures. Travis was honest enough to remind us that some other guy was also paralyzed playing hockey in the same rink less than a year later—but no one even remembers that guy's name.

"Let me tell you about Jeffrey," I said.

And so I repeated the argument as I had told it to our doctors one by one: Jeffrey in his long, terrible, anxious plummet, and then his sudden turnaround.

"For the first time in a long time, Jeff was beginning to be happy again," I told them. "And he was looking ahead to the future. And that was the moment when this accident had to happen. Of all the times it could have happened, it happened during the best week he had had in years, possibly the best day he had had in years.

"And," I said, "he will always believe he did it to himself. He wasn't struck by lightning or even a drunk driver. He dove into the pool himself. And if that isn't bad enough," I said, "he did it at the home of a psychiatrist. And his parents brought him back to life, to this condition we find him in.

"For all the rest of his life," I said, "Jeffrey will believe that he is the cause of his own paralysis. There is nothing anyone can say that will convince him otherwise. He will always believe that, and he will always be tormented by it."

"I am fifty-two years old," I told the group. "When Jeff is forty, I will be seventy-five years old. I don't know how long Toby and I will be able to handle Jeff at home, even if we have help. The folks at the rehab hospitals tell us it is pretty hard. At some point, Jeffrey is going to have to go somewhere else. There is no good place for him to go. By the time other kids in Jeff's generation are just hitting their peak, with careers and families and homes of their own, Jeff will long since have been delivered into the hands of strangers.

"Some of you," I said, "are probably concerned about the timing of our decision. Jeffrey is going to be eighteen in November. In only a few months the decision will be entirely his, not ours. So why are we so willing to make the decision now?

"Well," I said, "we consider this to be a window of opportunity that will close soon. Right now, he is in the intensive care unit. If we make the decision to pull his life support, it can happen. If we wait until Jeffrey is eighteen, he will be in a rehabilitation hospital or at home. If he then makes the decision that he would rather die, *how does that decision get carried out?* Jeff can't remove himself from his own life support. If I do it, I will probably be subject to criminal prosecution. And is there any doctor here who would bring Jeffrey in as a patient for the sole purpose of killing him?"

No one raised a hand.

"We are ready to make the decision ourselves," I said. "But we don't have to do anything about it today. Jeff has just had his tracheostomy tube installed. We are just becoming able to talk to him in a meaningful way. I think I know how he would decide this issue, but we want to take some time over the next few days. I want to talk to him and listen to him and see how he is responding to all of this. He may surprise me. He may be turning into a different Jeffrey than the one I knew."

I told the ethics committee that, as far as we parents were concerned, this meeting represented the last necessary level of review within the hospital. If and when we indicated the time had come to execute our decision, I did not expect that any further reconsideration would be necessary.

At some point I just stopped talking. I don't know how long I had rambled on. I do know that a few of the people in the room were crying. Even Dr. Duncan had a tear or two, I think.

Dr. Forman told us that we seemed to have covered a lot of territory in a few days. He suggested opening the meeting to questions.

Just then someone came in and told us that Jeffrey was calling for us—that he was frantic. Another conversation interrupted. Ed Forman told us the committee would discuss the matter in private and would ask us to meet with them again if they had issues to pursue.

As I was leaving, one of the doctors told me she was surprised at how well prepared we had been. It seemed we had anticipated all of her primary concerns and had responded to each in a clearheaded way.

I told her something an old friend had once told me: sometimes you have to lie to enhance your credibility. "How do you know I meant everything I said?" I asked her. "How could you know if I was just telling you what I thought you wanted to hear?"

As I spoke to her, I became truly emotional for the first time that day. During the meeting, I was calm and could meet every person's stare with confidence. But in the face of this compliment for a job well done, I began to cave in.

"You have to understand," I told the doctor, "I hate having to go through this. I hate having to figure out what I have to do to get this thing done. This is what I do for a living, and I hate using the same stuff when I'm talking about my son."

Jeffrey Benjamin Robot

I wasn't prepared for the Jeffrey I found waiting for us after we left the ethics committee meeting. Jeff had become a robot in agony. He was still very much under the influence of his medication. His voice was flat and monotonic, yet it had a sharp electronic twang. He sounded as if he had spent a long time in an alien place and had come back with an accent.

"Get me up," he said. "Get me up, get me up."

He was in a dense fog of despair, and we struggled to break through, communicate, get him to respond.

"Please," he said.

"Please.

"Please."

Over and over the words would come, evenly spaced, as if by a slow metronome. Each word spoken exactly like the last, without any change in cadence or inflection, a flat twang.

"I'm going insane," he said.

"I'm going insane.

"I'm going insane."

He had been on his back, an invalid, for four days. He had not been able to turn his head even slightly to the side or to nod. As he came out of his drug-induced sleep this time, the rerecognition of his condition must have been overwhelming. He had to move. He had to sit up. In his strange voice, almost as if by incantation, he was begging us to lift him up.

"I need a boost," he said.

"I need a boost.

"I need a boost."

We tried to get through the haze and explain—again— why he had to stay the way he was. Trying to perk up his spirits, I promised him that I would find a way to rig him a TV. There was a large one mounted on the wall already, but not in Jeff's line of sight, which was determined by his halo vest. So that became my next project: for my paralyzed son, going insane in his bed, I would get a television.

Later that day, as he was coming out of another drug-induced sleep, he was a robot again.

"Open the door please," he said.

"Open the door please.

"Open the door please."

They were incantations.

"Get in the car.

"Get in the car.

"Get in the car."

His eyes weren't focusing on me or Toby—or on anything else. I got closer to him and tried to engage him.

"What car?" I asked. "What car do you want me to get in?"

He didn't know; he couldn't see the car.

"Sit in the car please," he said.

"Sit in the car please.

"Sit in the car please."

"Where should I sit?" I asked. "What seat should I sit in?" The driver's seat, he said. "What seat will you sit in?" I asked. The passenger seat, he said.

"Who is in the backseat?" No one.

"Where do you want the car to go?" Home.

"What will you do there?" Rest.

"What will you do after that?"

Watch TV.

Eat.

Anything.

Tell It Again

As Jeffrey's voice rose up, he tried to bring his body along. He could not get up. He was lying flat on his back again, as always. He asked, begged, pleaded with us to raise him up, help him sit up. As we explained why he couldn't get up, he began to remember that he was paralyzed.

He asked, "How did I get here?"

I asked him if he wanted the whole story again, and he said yes. It was four days after the accident; my son had been awake dozens of times and had met the horror of his condition dozens of times—and here we were, becoming newly acquainted with it once again, as always.

From reading the books by Christopher Reeve and Travis Roy, I learned that this is the way it will nearly always be for Jeff. In sleep, when he dreams, he may often be a whole person, with a whole person's capabilities and joys. But then dawn comes—or in Jeff's case, the drugs wear off—and the sleeper wakes to the fact of his paralysis. This can't be me, the waking sleeper says, this can't be my life.

Yes it can.

After I finished talking to Jeff about the accident and his condition, I asked him if he wanted me to tell him also about the future, his medical care and beyond. He said yes, and I started. But when I was telling him about the rehabilitation hospital, Jeff stopped me.

"Where will I go after that?" he asked.

"If Mom and I can take care of you, we will," I told him. "If our ability and your needs make it possible for you to live at home, then home is where you will live. If it isn't possible for you to live with us, we'll find another place where they can take care of you better. And we'll visit you and take you home on weekends and holidays and take you to movies—"

"You'll abandon me," he broke in.

"We'll never abandon you," I told him.

He didn't want to think about it anymore. He wanted to go to sleep again, but it was too soon. He began to sink, to fall back into that place—one stop short of consciousness—in which he floated so often. He began to chant again.

"I'm broken," he said. "Everything is broken; I broke it."

"I'm dying," he said. "I'm dying."

"You are not dying," I told him. "You are talking, and I am listening. That's what is going on, no more and no less."

I asked him if he would be happy living at home with his family, and he said yes.

I asked him if he could be happy living without the use of his legs and arms, and he said no.

"I was stupid," he said again. "I was stupid."

"Jeffrey," I asked, "when you dove into the pool, did you expect to hit the bottom?"

"No," he said.

"Well," I said, "if you expected to hit the bottom and you dove in anyway, that would have been stupid. But if you didn't expect to hit bottom when you dove in, that's different. That's bad luck."

"But I dove in," he said.

"Yes," I replied, "but if you walked across the street and you got hit by lightning, would you say you were stupid for walking across the street?"

"That's just talk," Jeffrey told me, ending the discussion.

And maybe it was. Maybe it was just talk. Maybe I was telling sweet lies to ease his pain. Maybe I didn't believe a word I told him. Maybe it was all just empty, phony talk.

But how interesting: My ruined, drugged-up, robot son had begun to probe my words for bullshit.

....

Words simply cannot suffice to express our emotions at this time. Please know that we are thinking of you constantly and hope that somehow everybody's collective prayers and support can comfort you.—WILEEN SNOW

....

The Usual Suspect: God

This is what was missing from our crisis: someone to negotiate with.

"I'll settle for breathing and his arms," I said to Toby one day, out of the blue, with no prologue.

"So would I," she replied at once, as if she had been thinking the very same thing.

It was a fact that we couldn't settle, but it was also a fact that we felt a powerful *need* to settle. There was this awful, nagging feeling that there ought—there just plain *ought* —to be someone in authority who could broker the future for us, if we were reasonable about the terms.

But there never was. There was no one to convince, persuade, or even buy off. There was nothing we could tender in exchange for a different outcome. Not love. Not money. Not even our lives. We had nothing to trade and no one to barter with.

During this period of desperate choices and desolation, some people predictably suggested that we barter with God. They put it differently, of course. They talked about the power of prayer. Good people wrote to me or spoke to me about the power of prayer. I was usually respectful of their beliefs, and only occasionally resistant. I realized that prayer had terrific power to comfort those who believed in it, and I was happy for the solace it gave to them. Personally, I had no tolerance for dogma.

It would have been nice to have someone to negotiate with, but I wasn't going to bargain with someone else's fantasy.

"Thank God I have no religion!" I used to tell people. Most people got the point, and others needed only a gentle explanation. I believed in a world of chance, of good luck and bad luck. Chance put Jeffrey where he was, not anyone's God.

To me, Jeffrey's accident was an accident and no more. Horrible, but an accident only. If he had won the lottery, I would not have labeled it a miracle.

"I'm not angry at anyone," I could say, honestly. I believed that no one intended Jeffrey to be destroyed, no one—mortal or otherwise. I did not blame God. I had no need to imagine a God so that I could imagine the blame.

In fact, I would have become enraged at anyone willing to accept Jeff's injury as something less than *absolutely* horrible. Heaven help the guy who tells me it's all part of God's plan. For that matter, heaven help the God.

Once or twice, when his parents were not present, people visiting Jeffrey told him he should pray if he wanted to get better. I used to think, Is there a God so petty and so vain that he would torment Jeffrey to win respect or fear or to wring a prayer out of someone? Was God that much of a bully? Was some God using Jeff as an example to others, as a teaching tool? An example of what, teaching what? Could God be so clumsy in his educational technique? And if this was part of "God's plan," then I had to question his sanity. Is there a rational deity who could have left paralysis *out* of the mix but instead decided to keep it *in*?

Imagine Creation: "Okay," said God, "I'll give them butterflies and rainbows and puppy dogs and laughter, and ... Hmm, what's missing? ... Oh, right! I forgot quad-riplegia!"

Inner Circles

That evening the unparalyzed members of the family had a rare talk together. Sarah was feeling quite left out of things. She had been dropping in for visits with her host families, but she seemed to be hearing about Jeff from others and felt bad that she knew less than they did. I explained to her that lots of people came and went, and we were answering the same questions over and over, and if she was in the room she got the same information the others got. I told her if she had any questions, she should ask us, and we would tell her the same thing we told any of the others.

Then I told her about the inner circle. "There are some things," I said, "that are discussed only in a smaller, private group. Just Mom and I, Jeff, and our advisers. There are some things about Jeff's condition, his treatment, and other issues that we don't discuss with anybody else. That's just the way it has to be for now.

"But I promise you," I said, "every single thing I tell any of our friends and relatives, I am willing to tell you. If you don't hear about something, it's only because you weren't there when someone asked a question and we answered it, or because you didn't ask yourself."

Sarah wanted to know more about the inner circle. "Does Jeffrey know everything?" she asked. "Do you talk to him about everything?"

"No," I said. "There are some things we don't talk about even with Jeffrey, at least right now."

"So," she said, "there are really *two* inner circles. And I'm not in either of them."

"I guess you're right," I said, and thought, Not bad; smart kid.

....

I remember Jeffrey from before he was born. All that love and nurturing he has always been showered with will get him through . . . If sheer love can do it, he will be okay and use his life well . . . I will ask my community, St. Francis Chapel, to pray for Jeff and all of you . . . I believe group prayer is very powerful.—BARBARA GIANOLA

....

Thursday, July 9

....

ON THURSDAY MORNING I TOOK A CLUMSY SHOWER, without soap, in the small bathroom off the parents' lounge. I was still wet when a nurse told us Jeffrey was awake. He was asking if he was paralyzed. He was asking if he would ever walk. He wanted to see himself in the mirror.

He did not want to see his parents.

I began to wonder, Has the staff been talking to him about us? Is he now frightened of us, as he is frightened about so many other things?

A while later, the nurse came back and told us Jeff had quieted down and would see us. When we arrived at his room, Dr. Duncan was talking to the staff about problems with Jeffrey's ventilator. Jeff was experiencing "air hunger." He felt as if he were suffocating, although the vent machine was working fine.

The staff considered options. There were variables to coordinate: setting the volume (the amount of air per puff), the rate (puffs per minute), and the expansion of the tracheostomy tube's inflatable cuff. Depending on how they adjusted the interrelated variables, Jeff might feel more comfortable, but he might lose his voice.

Jeff, naturally, made it known that he would rather breathe than talk.

I started to crater again. I needed Jeff's voice. I may have needed it more than Jeff did. Dr. Duncan assured us that in time the system would be tuned properly and Jeff would be able to speak. It might happen right away, or it might take a few weeks.

"I understand," I told Dr. Duncan privately, "but you know I need to talk to Jeff over the next few days." There were decisions to execute or not.

It had been about five days since the accident. It had been about three days since Toby and I began actively considering Option Two, and Dr. Snelling had cautioned us that the decision would get harder the longer we waited. I was feeling the pressure of time. I felt weighed down by it, physically burdened by it. Time had become a tangible thing to be coped with, carried, like a basket of bricks.

I needed to talk to Jeff. I needed to listen to him. When I heard that his voice would be cut off, it hurt. It would slow things down. And because "speaking" without a voice would be difficult for Jeff, he would not want to talk very much.

The Opportunity to Wait

A while later, in a quiet corner of the intensive care unit, a short conversation took place. It lasted less than three minutes, but it affected the outcome of Jeff's stay more than any other conversation to that point.

A doctor who had heard about Option Two said to me, "I understand that you believe there is a 'window of opportunity' for deciding on life support, and that if Jeffrey goes home, the opportunity will be lost, even after he becomes an adult. Am I right? Is that one of the reasons why you feel you have to decide the issue right away?"

"You're right," I told him.

"What if your assumption is wrong?" he asked. "What if there were a facility or a practice that would be willing to accept Jeffrey as a patient and honor his request if he makes it? Would that be important to your decision?"

I barely paused before I answered him.

"I am not afraid to make the decision now," I said. "But I understand that it is Jeffrey's decision we are making. So the answer is yes. That would be very important."

"Well," he said, "I would like to assure you that Jeffrey would have that option as an adult. If you are interested, I would have to confirm one or two things. Could you wait a little while?"

"Yes, I could," I told him. He left, and I made the transition from hell to limbo.

After that short meeting, I returned to Jeff's room. He wanted to see a mirror again. We now had a large rectangular mirror, much bigger than the little one I had used the first time. He got quite a look. He asked me, much more quickly than before, to put the mirror away.

"I'm so sad," he told me. "Why did I dive into the pool? Why did I do that?"

"You did it to have fun," I replied.

"Will I be paralyzed?"

"Yes."

"Forever?"

"Yes, that's what the doctors tell us."

"No basketball?"

"No basketball."

"No driveway hoop?"

"That's right."

He began to cry again. We had already had this conversation once before. He had already cried when we had it. Now he was there again, learning the same sad news again. His face contorted, unnaturally because of the steel screws fixed to his brow. A teardrop formed at the outer corner of his near eye, and as it started to run down his cheek, I captured it with my finger.

He needed a hug but couldn't be hugged. Our arms were not long enough to hug him. Our arms were not long enough to reach around the bed, the rails, the rods, the tubes, the wires . . . and Jeff.

Exchanging Hats

Later I was in a small room alone. Linda Goodale, a child life specialist (a highly qualified scrounger and enabler), came in and asked if Jeffrey would like a quilt made by members of the Linus Club.

"Are they affiliated with any religion?" I asked.

"No," she said. "It's just a group of people who make quilts for folks who are in the hospital. If you would like to, you can pick one out for Jeffrey. If you feel uncomfortable, you don't have to."

"Why don't you pick one out for me?" I asked her. She was holding a sample, and I pointed to it. "Why not that one?" I said.

"Well, it might be too small," she said, unfolding it.

Too small for the whole body, I thought, but not for the part that can still feel warm and cold. I told her, "Go ahead and pick out any other."

"Does he have a favorite color?" she asked me.

I broke down again. I had to make so many choices for Jeffrey. Did I have to choose his colors too? What color did he like? I didn't know what color he liked. He liked snowboarding. Did she have a snowboarding quilt? Crying came so quickly now. Suddenly, out of nowhere. Like dust devils or squalls.

She patted my head to comfort me. I recovered too quickly. "Believe me," I said. "I'm okay now. I've learned how."

And it was true. I could recover in seconds. It was a new

skill I had learned to deal with the situation. I couldn't always hold back the tears, but I could usually shut them off when I needed to. I would be crying and say to the person with me, "I'm going to put one of my other hats on now. Watch me." And over the course of a few seconds, I could sniffle, pick up my head, flash a practiced smile, and be some other creature.

A visitor would walk into the lounge, a fellow I had played golf with a time or two, and I would remember in a rush: Jeff had just gotten interested in golf. I had just bought him a set of clubs. We had just started playing at a local public course. And now . . .

The emotion would come over me like a sudden fever, and I would cry. Someone would pat me on the back. Then a nurse or a doctor would come in and ask to see me about a medical issue. In the time it took to walk the few steps into the ICU, I had calmed and dried myself and was ready to do business.

When Toby and I drove to one of the rehab hospitals, I emitted faint moans all the way and frequently had to swab my eyes for tears. There was no need to stop moaning, and so I couldn't stop. I just let the sorrow fill me up and overflow. Then, as I parked the car in the lot, I said to Toby, "Time to put on my administrative hat," and the emotional grip loosened immediately. I wiped my eyes, reached for my notebook, and was transformed. By the time we reached the front door, you might have thought I was there to read the electric meter.

Friday, July 10

·····································

MICHAEL GOLDSTEIN ARRIVED WITH DOCUMENTS HE
had downloaded from Web sites of the National Spinal
Cord Injury Association and a rehabilitation hospital spe-
cializing in spinal cases. Other people had been Web
surfing too. I told them to give me anything they found. I
would do my homework before going to sleep at night.

Also, each night, I had begun to make notes in my red
three-ring binder. It had become a kind of diary and a
form of therapy. Recording events and developing my

thoughts had a way of soothing me at night, like warm milk.

Unfortunately, I found that even in the quietest moments, when I was alone and time whispered tranquilly along, both my spirits and my handwriting were haggard and distressed. I had deteriorated. I would scrawl letters and words that I didn't recognize even as I put them onto paper. When I tried to write *national* it came out *natonola*.

The Gospel According to Mr. Parker

I met with Jeff's psychiatrist, Dr. Gregory Fritz. He had been assigned by the hospital to help Jeff get through the ordeal. As a by-product, he ended up counseling us parents as well. And as an extra-special added bonus, I got to torture Dr. Fritz. Today was relatively easy for him. We concentrated on why, precisely, I was so willing to kill my son.

"Davy Crockett," I told Dr. Fritz. "I am a card-carrying member of the Davy Crockett generation." I recalled for Dr. Fritz the evenings long ago when I had sat in a chair, eating popcorn and watching TV, and Fess Parker—the actor playing Davy Crockett—had laid down the rule by which I, my generation, and all men must live: *"Be sure you're right—then go ahead."*

Some Disney hack back in the fifties whacked out a script a week; a line got spoken by a second-rate actor in a coonskin hat; and because it was simple enough for a ten-year-old to understand and remember, here I was at age fifty-two, ready to do the unthinkable.

"Be sure you're right—then go ahead."

I was actually quoting Davy Crockett—the gospel according to Fess—to a pedigreed doctor of psychiatric medicine. I was not quoting Scripture because—I told Dr. Fritz and everyone else—religion was not sufficiently *rational* for me.

Colleagues Bearing Gifts and Burdens

I was visited by Gary St. Peter and John Tarantino. We three were law partners once, in one of the larger Providence firms. I left to start a new, small practice, and soon after, Gary left to do the same thing. The people we left at the firm were our friends, however, and we had all stayed friends over the intervening years. Gary and John asked to meet with Toby and me in the hospital's small conference room.

"A few days ago," Gary said, "we opened a bank account for Jeffrey. We are going to set up a trust, and we are going to ask for contributions.

"Every partner and former partner we have contacted has already contributed," John said. They told us an architectural firm had offered to work with us—without a fee—on home modifications, and a construction company had offered to help.

I was thunderstruck, but most of all I had to apologize.

"I am sorry," I told them. "I should be falling down crying out of gratitude. But I can't. I promised myself I would not think about or talk about money right now. I haven't looked at our medical insurance; I tell providers I don't want to hear about costs. What you are doing is wonderful, and I can't tell you how much it means to us. And I should be dissolving into a puddle of gratitude, but I can't."

They understood. But not quite.

"I hope you guys are keeping track of everyone's name and address," I said.

Of course they were. They even had a committee, with meetings scheduled. They were planning fund-raising events.

I asked if I should attend the meetings. They said they wouldn't let me.

"You know," I told them, "this isn't over, here. There's no guarantee Jeffrey is going to make it out of this place."

They said they understood. But not quite. They didn't know, not quite.

"I have a hard time believing all this," I told them. "I'm not a prominent guy. I keep a pretty low profile. Why would a contractor I don't know want to do a job for me?"

"In part because people who know you are calling in some favors," they said. "And in part it's because some people just plain want to help. There are a lot of them."

They began to tell me about phone calls and meetings, people who spent time crying in their offices when they heard the news. People who had started minicampaigns to chase down help for us, without our knowing they were doing it, how, or with whom.

This I did not expect. This I had not factored into the mix. Committees being formed. Contributions made. Arms being twisted, or heartstrings pulled.

My family had become a corporation. Tragedy, Incorporated. Quadriplegia, Inc.

Until now, Toby and I could look around, and everyone involved in the decision was within our reach: our family, our close friends, the medical staff. We knew everyone involved in the actions we would take; everyone from whom an emotional, personal reaction could be expected; and everyone to whom an apology might someday have to be given.

Now, as the news from John and Gary began to sink in, I realized that we were the center of more than one circle. The outer orbit, formed by the gravity of our predicament, was larger than I had realized.

Who were all these people? How would we cope with them?

A short time later, both Toby and I met with Dr. Fritz. I told him about the trust and the efforts being organized by Gary and John.

"Everyone needs to believe there's going to be a good end to this," I said. "Everyone feels compassion for us. They want to help. They want to believe their help will make a difference. More than anything, they want to believe things will turn out right."

I asked Dr. Fritz to imagine what would happen now if we turned off Jeffrey's life support.

"When we started this," I said, "I knew we would have to convince a lot of people. Everybody has a point of view. Everybody has a different way of looking at things. I found myself having to say something different to everyone. With every person, I had to find a different argument, a different line of reasoning. One by one, I had to figure out what works.

"I always knew we would have to carry a lot of people on our shoulders," I said, beginning to cry. "But I never expected we would have to carry the whole damn state."

Trust Me

Jeff was awake and willing to talk. He wanted to get out of his bed and out of his halo. I told him that lying there was the first skill he had to learn if he wanted to get better. He told me how hard it was.

He had not become accustomed to the tracheostomy tube, which had been cut into his lower throat. His mechanical ventilator pushed air through the tube, bypassing his nose and mouth, so Jeff didn't get the normal sensation of breathing. He felt as if he were choking.

I told him, "Don't worry. *You can't choke.* Trust me. The air you need goes through the tube into your lungs. Even if you can't feel it, the machine is doing its job. When fluid builds up in your throat, you feel like you're choking. It's a natural response. You just have to convince yourself that you aren't actually choking.

"It's a skill. Reinterpreting that feeling is a skill. Pushing it out of your mind is a skill. You'll eventually get used to it."

I left feeling satisfied that I had calmed his fears and made his new life that much more tolerable. All it needed was a clear explanation, I reminded myself; take out the mystery, and these problems could be managed.

A few hours later, a nurse told me there had been an emergency. A mucus plug had formed in the tracheostomy tube, shutting off Jeff's air supply and sounding alarms. A crew responded quickly, using a rugged ambulation bag—a flexible, football-shaped air pump—to ventilate Jeff by hand while the problem was fixed. Jeff had been terrified.

Just this morning I had told him something like this could not happen. I was stupid. I did not know. I lied to him by telling him things I had no right to say. I would have to be more careful. He would have to trust me less, and so would I.

TV or Not TV

Over the past couple of days I had been spending much of my time trying to put a television set where Jeff could see it. I had spoken to four men working in various hospital departments. Each had given me a somewhat different take on the rules governing what electronic equipment could be brought into the intensive care unit. The hospital's own TVs were specially wired, tested, and certified for ICU use. Uncertified equipment could emit radiation or contribute to power surges, interfering with life support or monitoring systems.

I had to find something that ran on batteries or a twelve-volt converter and could be hung or tabled above Jeff's bed, just a few inches from his head.

So I had been making phone calls and running around, trying to find a table, a TV, wiring, connectors, and switches that would permit me to put a small screen directly in Jeff's line of vision. I had been to seven different electronics stores, some of them more than once, looking for a combination that would work.

So many visits to electric wonderlands. From Jeff, clinging to the basics of food, water, and air . . . to consumer paradise, with hundreds of glimmering screens, illuminating the enticements of a larger life.

Images flickered everywhere. The women were beautiful, the men were fit, the explosions were magnificent, and everyone breathed without a machine.

In one store, a man debated whether a sixty-inch screen was large enough for him, while I was looking at a thirteen-inch model and thinking, Too big, too big. I resigned myself grudgingly to a nine-inch set and eventually had to settle for a five-inch.

Settle . . . I had to settle. Whatever was not too big or too small or too high or too low or too far left or right. From the infinite variety of options, I would have to pick only the one that was adaptable to Jeff's particular capabilities and needs.

I realized as I considered this, driving back to the hospital with his midget TV in the trunk, that I had begun to mix up Jeff's losses with my own. After all, shouldn't whatever worked for Jeff be enough for me as well?

Linda Goodale, the child life specialist, helped me search for a table or stand on which to place the little TV. She took me to a supply room full of parts, connectors, and miscellaneous fragments of things. Linda had

seen me fooling with the TV wiring, switching out ca-
bles and splicing in pieces I had bought at RadioShack.
On our way to the supply room, Linda remarked that I
seemed to know a lot about mechanical things. I told
her that all my life I had been a tinkerer. I loved projects
of all kinds, I told her. I loved to make things and to fix
things.

"But you can't fix this," she said. "Can you?"

"No," I said, "I can't fix this."

Linda found a nice metal table we could use. The legs
rolled on casters and would fit under the bed. The tabletop
would clear Jeff's chest and all the tubes. That night, I was
off to Home Depot for some poplar and hardware, then
back to my house to use the shop tools. I made a cradle
with adjustable legs so that the TV could be held tightly in
place on the table, and the screen could be tilted up or
down to point straight into Jeffrey's eyes. He would be
able to look squarely into a five-inch screen from a distance of less than a foot.

The contraption finally done, I went back to the hospital. We locked the TV and cradle into place with duct tape,
ran the cabling and patched it into the hospital's VCR system, and finally popped in a movie. Everything worked. I
was proud.

Ten minutes later, Jeff was asking for drugs so that he
could go to sleep again. He had barely lasted through the
movie's opening credits. When the nurse came in to clear
his tracheostomy tube, to help him fall asleep, Jeff told her
he felt like he was in the pool again, drowning.

WHILE TALKING TO a visitor on Friday, I absentmindedly pulled up my pant leg and gently scratched my knee. No . . . wait . . . I was picking at a scab. I hadn't noticed it before.

Apparently, my knee had been scraped while I was pulling Jeff out of the water or kneeling on the concrete apron to revive him. Seeing my own insubstantial wound, I remembered that Jeff had a similar scrape on his left shoulder. The staff had covered it with some kind of transparent bandage, and I could tell it had been regularly medicated. The hospital treated all of Jeff's wounds; mine was healing on its own.

In the crisis on July 4, I had suffered an *abrasion,* and Jeff's spine had suffered a *contusion.* They both sounded insignificant. There ought to be more grandeur to Jeff's injury. Cancer, now there's something with resonance.

What happened to your son? He jumped into a pool and got a *contusion.*

It doesn't resonate.

What happened to your son? He got *cancer.*

See? Given the consequences, *cancer* sounds a lot better.

I read that Jeff's injury is called the hangman's break because it is exactly the kind of fracture that an executioner has in mind when he sets the knot just so on the condemned convict's neck. When the felon drops through the gallows floor, his neck bones snap around the C1-C2 level. The convict suffers a mean contusion up near the top of the spine, just about where Jeffrey suffered his, and the witnesses watch him die. The convict's father doesn't jump in and breathe for him, the EMTs don't ventilate him on the way to the hospital, and the surgeons don't set his neck into a halo vest. No.

The hanging isn't the cause of death. It's the neglect that follows the hanging. Maybe they could bring them all back to life if they wanted to. After all, it's only a little bruise.

....

I have been attempting to sit down and write this letter for a week now and find I still don't know what to say. To say that I understand your grief is not possible, but I can say that my thoughts are with you and you have many friends who are constantly thinking about you.—ALAN LITWIN

....

Becoming a Legend

I said to Jeff more than once that a million kids could jump into that pool and come out nothing but wet. I could also have said—but did not—that some of them might have suffered scrapes, broken fingers, broken noses, concussions, brain damage, and death. Chance presents a variety of outcomes.

Especially for the young, the pursuit of fun is very often the pursuit of danger. A hospital visitor told me—he shuddered as he remembered it—that some kids he knew used to jump into their family's pool *from the roof of their house.*

Judging from the reports of our visitors, our mail, and our answering machine, Jeff's accident had become the talk of the town. It seemed everyone knew about it and was anguished. A lawyer friend told me that even at work, almost every discussion or phone call started or ended with mention of Jeffrey. Everyone was talking about it. Everyone was telephoning everyone else.

I was beginning to understand why. Our luck was so devastatingly bad that it had maxed out the parental terror meter. A kid dives into a pool, interrupts dinner, and ends up paralyzed forever. How's *that* for a conversation starter?

My world had become smaller over the past few days, and I had lost touch with the larger network of life, the hive of our community. It was buzzing. In one week, we had become a legend. We had become the standard against which tragedies could now be measured.

I told someone that twenty years from now, parents would warn their kids to wear their helmets, use their seat belts, or stay away from drugs because "if you don't listen to me, you'll end up like Jeffrey Galli."

"Everyone is talking about it," a friend told me. "They're all upset."

"Tell them not to worry," I replied. "Statistically, we've taken the pressure off everybody else."

Another friend tried to console me. "No one could expect this," he said. "What are the odds against something like this?"

"Well," I replied, "statistically the accident never happened."

Three young men came into the family lounge. One was Jeff's oldest friend, Chris St. Peter, who had come to visit. The other two were just tagging along with Chris. One of them was using crutches and had a heavy cast on his right leg.

"What happened to you?" I asked.

"I broke my leg playing soccer," he replied.

"You know," I told him, "you ought to stick to low-impact sports. Like *swimming*."

....

The news of the accident left us reeling . . . On the one hand, there's so much I'd like to tell you, and on the other hand, words fail me completely. I will just say that I do believe prayer makes a difference, and as often as I think about you—which is very often— I am praying for each one of you . . . Don't let go.—SANDY FEIT

I saw Jeff—basically my visit put him to sleep . . . Anyway—I left you pizza and cookies. Heat pizza in microwave to make it taste good. We love you both very much.—BARBARA HARRIS

....

Saturday, July 11

....

SATURDAY MORNING CAME. ANOTHER DREAMLESS NIGHT. I woke up knowing only that life had been suspended for a while, and that Jeff was paralyzed. It is Saturday, and I am alive, I thought. I am compelled to be alive. If I am alive tomorrow, blame compulsion.

I was alone. Toby was already up. She is definitely a morning person. Before the accident, every day she would rise early and take Kirby for a long run. I would usually be up later at night, watching TV or working on the computer, and would rise later than she. Now, at the hospital, I would stay up later, reading or writing, and she always woke up before I did. Amazing how the rhythms of our former life tried to maintain their hold. I tried to organize my mind and resolved to meet the new day.

Chalices and Cans of Beer, Veneration and Delight

I began thinking of Jeffrey eating steak. Lately Jeff had been asking if he would be able to eat normal food. We didn't know. He had to make progress in small steps. First, he had to sit up; he had to get used to his tracheostomy tube; he had to be tested. If he could not control his swallowing, and the food leaked into his lungs (they call it aspiration), he would be unable to eat real food. He might be able to eat processed food, like baby food, but not, for example, steak.

Jeffrey loved steak. He would often make it himself on our outdoor grill. Sometimes, when Toby was out for the night, I would get Jeff a steak even when Sarah and I were eating something else.

I remember the moves he would make in a cooking process that had become a ritual.

Through the back door, onto the deck. Light the grill, come back.
Open the package to reveal the meat. Onto the plate.

Back through the door, in and out, and back again.
Turning, checking, cooking.
Lift the lid. Squeeze the tongs. Turn. Sizzle. Feel the
heat, feel the oily smoke.
Get the sauce. Unscrew the cap. Tap onto the plate.
Preparation. Anticipation. Familiar motion. Pleasure.

A Latin phrase percolated up from the depths of my
memory: "Ad Deum, qui laetificat juventutem meam."
They were the first words spoken by the altar boy at the
opening of a Latin Mass. My mind wandered back to
boyhood. I didn't last long in altar boy training. But I remember the attraction. The ritual of the Latin Mass was
wonderful in its poetic blending of movement and sound:
the elevation of the chalice by a person whose robed arms
dripped red and golden fabric; the tinkling of a bell and
the bellow of an organ; and people kneeling and rising on
cue. A person could become enthralled by the Mass without knowing the significance of any part of it, without understanding a single word. That was the awful, beautiful
power of its ritual.

Now I was thinking of another ritual: Jeffrey making a
steak and eating what he had made. As I thought of all the
separate steps that Jeffrey used to combine into the litany
of his meal, I wondered at the spiritual content inhabiting
our movements.

There is a spiritual side to physical action. Ritual—any
kind of ritual—is largely physical. And the physical things
we do—the movements we make that serve us in life and

give us pleasure—these movements become a kind of ritual on which our spiritual life depends whether we know it or not.

I began to understand, at last, why I was so distraught over Jeffrey's paralysis. It was not just action he would lack. It was the spiritual fulfillment that comes from action. Our limbs are connected to our souls as well as to our brains.

Among the movements of life that have meaning, there are these: To bow a head; to kneel; to raise the Eucharist. To elevate the Torah scroll; to throw the candy at the new Bar Mitzvah. To throw the rice at the newlyweds. To make the sign of the cross; to carry the casket; to sprinkle soil on the grave.

But there are these as well: To swing a five iron smoothly and with grace. To roll a ball down an echoing lane. To scoop a grounder, twist, and toss to second. To flip a rod, to slice a backhand, or to skate into a spin.

To fit a dress to a daughter's waist. To knot a son's necktie and snug it to his collar. To pat the dog that has caught the ball. To toast the honored guest. To salute the flag. To touch a shoulder gently.

There is a spiritual aspect of physical movement that no combination of wires and switches can possibly replace. There is a spirituality to the movement of our hands and limbs that no mechanical, electric proxy can provide.

To shake a hand in greeting or wave good-bye. To embrace in happiness, in loving, or in grief. To cook a steak and cut it into pieces. Movement can be glorious. In a church, in a temple, in a kitchen; it's glorious; it's life.

Lying in a visitors' lounge made gray by blinds I chose not to open, I thought of how unsatisfying life had become. I could not bear to think of Jeffrey eating steak ground into mush or cut into little bits. Steak in a spoon held in someone else's hand.

The loss of Jeff's physical potential had taken the joy out of mine. I probably would not install the basketball hoop. I might not play tennis this year. I didn't care.

It was just simply, unalterably true that continuing to live did not appear to be a satisfying option. This was not a question of strength or courage. It was a question that came naturally if you believed life is always a choice and not just a condition.

My mind played over the landscape of this new, week-old world and pronounced it an unsatisfactory place in which to build a satisfactory future.

Toby came in, wondering why I had lingered so long alone. Jeffrey had been up and alert while I had been musing. She told me Jeff was not in a positive mood. He said he was a wimp. He said he wanted to die. He said he had had a nightmare about Christopher Reeve.

Toby began crying more despondently than usual. We talked about the decision, Option Two. It was still hanging there, like a bomb with a dampened fuse.

With the advent of the trust, death had become harder to contemplate. There were so many people—some of whom we didn't even know—who were making an investment in the outcome. "Make sure you save the names and addresses," I had told Gary and John when they broke the news. They were probably thinking of thank-you cards.

I was too, but I was also wondering if we would have to send the contributions back.

I could imagine the note. Here's your money back. Thanks, but we killed our kid.

Bedridden Boredom

When I finally saw Jeff later that morning, he was watching a movie. He desperately needed anchors to the world. First it was his parents. Now, and increasingly, it was entertainment—music and television. He seemed to be interested in the movie. From time to time he commented on the action. When the film was nearly over, as the action was becoming frantic, Jeff gave up and asked for drugs so that he could fall asleep again. I asked him if the two of us could talk before he slept, while the nurse was getting him ready.

He told me this must all be boring for us. I assured him it was quite the opposite of boring; every night I was exhausted.

I asked him what he had dreamed about the night before. "What's this about Christopher Reeve?" Jeff had forgotten, exactly, although he did remember telling his mom he might direct a movie some day. Christopher Reeve had done that. Reeve was paralyzed, and he seemed to be doing okay, Jeff said.

I asked Jeff to try something with me: I asked him to try to remember some of the things he liked to do that involved the mind most of all and didn't require too much of the body. I figured he would mention surfing the Net, watching movies, drawing, and retouching photos on the computer.

He couldn't think of anything.

"Well," I said, "I remember you used to read *Newsweek* a lot."

"That's boring," Jeff told me.

"I'm surprised you think it's boring," I said, "since you spent so much time doing it."

"It wasn't boring then," Jeff told me. "It's boring now."

I ruminated on that. *Newsweek* to Jeffrey would have represented not just intellectual gratification or the love of language or current events, but also a vast menu of opportunities and experiences, most of which Jeff would no longer be able to enjoy. Cars. Girls. Everything.

Jeff asked again— *again*— that I tell him how the accident had happened. I condensed it: "You fell or dove into the pool. The kids came up to the house and told us you were underwater and not moving. Mom and I went down to the pool and saw you—"

He stopped me.

"I remember," he said. "I remember being underwater."

"Do you remember drowning?" I asked. "Do you remember looking up and seeing the sky above the water?"

"No," he said. "I remember being underwater; then I must have passed out."

"We pulled you out," I continued. "We revived you. I couldn't use your mouth, so I breathed through this." I touched his nose. "You probably don't remember drowning because the accident injured your spine, and you couldn't breathe. So I guess your lungs didn't take in a lot of water, and that made it easier for me to push the air into them. It would have been worse if your lungs had been full of water."

"That was lucky," Jeff said matter-of-factly.

"When we pulled you out, your eyes were wide-open and staring straight ahead. As I breathed into you, I could see them change. I could see you coming back to us."

"I guess I was lucky," Jeff said again.

He again told me that I must be bored, that this whole process must be "a pain in the butt."

"It's nothing," I said, "compared to raising babies. When a baby is young, it always cries when you want to sleep. You used to puke all over us after we fed you, and then after puking you would cry to eat some more."

He smiled.

"Will I be able to have kids?" he asked.

"Not the usual way," I told him. We talked about the facts: a child is made by the meeting of a sperm and an egg. Children would be possible, I said, even if the usual method of arranging the meeting were not.

Jeff said, "Maybe they'll find a cure. Maybe some day they can cure me."

We could always hope for that, I said.

Walking Business

We started to watch another movie. A comedy, a good one. Jeff watched an actor cross the screen.

"I wish I could walk like that," he said.

"Well," I said, "to do it like that, you'll have to take years of acting lessons." He laughed a little.

There was a point to his comment. Jeff had begun to evaluate what he saw according to what he had lost. To me, there was nothing special about the fact that a character moved a few steps from point *A* to point *B*. To Jeff, the action was special—desirable, in fact. Even *enviable*.

I imagined a movie script: Nicholson enters from right, walks to door, in doing so making entire audience hunger for more walking business.

On Saturday night, Jeff was full of questions: What was his sleeping drug called? How did they get it in him? What was a bolus? (It's the initial "shot" of drug, given at the start of an intravenous transfusion.) We and the nurse tried to explain things to him.

"Interesting," he said.

Then he wanted to know if insurance was paying for everything. I told him that when we fell short, we were going to search his bedroom for all his hidden cash.

And I told him that he owed us for the garbage. He didn't make it last Tuesday, I reminded him. He owed us three dollars. It could add up.

As the time neared for us to leave for the night, he started crying. The cuff of his tracheostomy tube was inflated, sealing his throat, so it was a soundless cry. Unable to cry with a voice, he did it purely with a heart-battering contortion of his face. Although the IV tubes were pumping him with fluid, he still had none to use for tears.

Two Jeffs

It had been a week since the accident. Jeff asked us if he would ever get out of the bed.

"Absolutely," I replied. "You'll be in a wheelchair before your birthday."

"That's good," he said. "That gives me hope."

So my son had hope. I did not ask—I was afraid to ask—what he hoped for.

One week after the accident, my son had hope when I had practically none. I was smart enough to know by now that his definition of *hope* was, and always would be, different from mine. I was smart enough to know that something he was hoping for might never be achieved. I was smart enough to know that his hope might rest on bad assumptions, faulty logic, or fantasy.

But I loved him enough to let him keep the hope he had.

Over the days, however few, I had come to understand that a new Jeffrey was being born. I had become the father of two Jeffs. Both births had been violent.

On November 26, 1980, Jeff had come to us by cesarean section. Doctors sliced open Toby's body and harvested Jeffrey, both mom and baby covered in gore. I was there, took pictures, and smiled.

This second birth involved less blood but a longer labor. The water had broken a week ago. Now he lay in his electrified, telemetric bed—his high-tech womb—surrounded by machines, plastic snakes, odd noises. Without moving an inch, Jeffrey was being reconstituted into a new being, one who might or might not be able to thrive in his new environment.

In one of my conversations with Dr. Fritz, the psychiatrist, I had said, "That isn't Jeffrey in there. That is a chrysalis. It is something turning into something else. We don't yet know what the new thing will be."

When Jeffrey was born the first time, he could do little more than twitch. He had age-appropriate wiggles in his trunk and limbs, but that isn't saying much. Without constant, vigilant care he would have died. It would be years before he could survive on his own.

Although utterly "normal," Jeff at birth was more vulnerable than the Jeff I looked upon in July 1998. Jeff the infant was less capable in most respects than Jeff the quadriplegic. At least the current Jeff could speak.

Baby Jeff could not walk, or drive a car, or make love to a sweetheart, or race a friend to the end of the pool. Neither could the current version of Jeff. But our Jeff, now, could talk. He could evaluate, instruct, and complain. He could communicate his love.

Between Jeff the baby and Jeff the quadriplegic, it was the *quad* who exhibited the greater capacity for self-determination.

So, I asked myself, why did I consider killing Jeffrey now, when I never would have considered it when he was small, devoid of real personality, and functionally useless? Why did I look at the helpless infant as a reservoir of hope, while in the boy in the bed I saw just a basket of hopelessness?

I knew the answer. Jeff's *potential* had been stolen from

him. Before the accident, both Jeffs—the baby and the adolescent—could paint a life with the same marvelous palette of potential. But the jump into the pool had washed it away.

Jeffrey had been suddenly and cruelly diminished. It was his *diminishment* that I could not bear to think about or to let him live to think about. I struggled against the conviction that a Jeffrey so diminished was worse than no Jeffrey at all.

On Saturday afternoon, when Jeff said the wheelchair would give him hope, I knew he was approaching a turning point. Would the hope give him strength, or would it eventually scald him with disappointment and despair? I didn't know.

I wouldn't push him. I would do what I had promised Dr. Duncan I would do. I would take some time to talk to Jeff, to listen, and to learn.

By the end of the day, I knew that I was moving in the direction of a big discussion with Jeff. I knew that Option Two would not be decided against him behind his back. I knew that Jeff was not going to die in this bed unaware of the possibility.

Saturday night I went to bed (well, okay, to the couch) still wondering if Jeff would live or die. But I also recognized that he was part of the decision—the most important part.

The Jeff who wanted to be drugged to sleep, who wanted to sleep through "everything," had gone away. This new Jeff also wanted to go to sleep and told us so. But this new Jeff wanted to know the name of the drug that would make the sleeping happen; he wanted to know the means of administering it and who was paying for it. This new Jeff wanted to go to sleep now simply because it was night. This new Jeff wanted to wake up in the morning.

And that began to seem important.

Sunday, July 12

·······························

IT WAS SUNDAY MORNING, AND A NURSE WOKE ME UP.

As I rose, I remembered part of the previous night's dream. In it, I was pestering Jeff about getting a summer job. Whom had he called, whom had he visited? He had to get a summer job.

Then I remembered that Jeff was paralyzed. Unlike the other mornings, this morning it took some time to remember that. This time, it was not the first thing I thought of. This time, I was disoriented. It took me twenty minutes to get up and put my shoes on.

·················

Perspective

Jeff and I started to watch a comedy. After drugs and air, and after his visitors, the TV and VCR had become Jeffrey's most important therapeutic aids.

When one of the characters (a rigid corporate type) did something predictably hostile, Jeff said, "That was stupid. He just fired the best man in the business."

Then, a few seconds later, Jeff said, "I take these movies too seriously. I keep commenting on them . . ."

At one point in the movie a woman undressed. She was blond, with very large breasts. "I like this part," Jeff said. "Wow . . . I like her."

We had seen the same film at home a year before. Then, he had remained absolutely silent during the sequence. Maybe he hadn't trusted me enough to comment; maybe he hadn't wanted his mother's attention drawn to the two guys ogling a naked blond in our den. Now he felt he had to say something. He had become so vocal about what he saw on TV. And he saw things so differently now.

When a character took a pratfall, Jeff didn't laugh.

"He could break his neck doing that," Jeff said, and then, "I hope I don't break my neck again."

At one point in another movie, the shooting of two people bothered him terribly. "I don't like to see that," he said. "I don't like to see violence."

Toby told me that the day before, Jeff had seen a man and a woman caressing, and he had said aloud, "I always dreamed of doing that."

Maintaining the Machinery

Jeff told me that his "volume" was down. I paused. Eight days before, Jeff would not have known what that term was supposed to mean. Today, even though he could not feel his lungs or see the ventilator, he sensed that there was a mechanical problem, something gone amiss with the volume controls.

I could not tell. I could see some gauges, but I couldn't see anything wrong. I consulted a nurse.

The nurse flipped a switch, and a readout displayed the volume. Jeff was correct. His volume was down. The nurse adjusted his tracheostomy tube, and the volume increased. The tube had settled out of position. That caused a leak or a constriction.

Before I ever did, Jeff had taken control of his mechanical life support. Eight days into his paralysis, he was beginning to teach me, and I was beginning to learn.

Cries and Echoes

"It's strange being numb all the time," Jeff said. "Sometimes I get surges, or tingles. I can't describe it. Now it's in my left leg, then it surges up and goes down into my right leg. It's probably my imagination."

I told him, "No, it may not be imagination. Remember that you feel things in your brain. You don't really feel things in your fingers or toes. Everything above the injury is still working. Your brain is sending out signals to your leg, looking for your leg. Your brain is trying to make the connection. That tingling you feel may be a kind of echo —your brain sending out a signal that bounces back."

"An echo," said the nurse. "What a great way of describing it."

She meant it as a compliment; it made me sad. I could imagine the lonely brain, sending signals, lighting flares, searching for the missing members of its squad.

When I saw him again later in the day, Jeffrey had earphones on and was listening to Gershwin.

"I remember listening to this in my room, with my feet up on my desk," he said. "I won't be able to do that anymore."

"Two out of three, Jeff," I said. "You will be able to listen to it in your room. You just won't have your feet on the desk."

"It won't be the same," Jeff said. "My feet will be bolted to a chair."

Eventually, he got weepy.

"It's so difficult," he said.

"It *is* difficult, Jeff," I replied. "It would be difficult for everyone in your position. It's difficult because it is, not because you're a wimp or a coward."

I couldn't tell if he even nodded. I couldn't tell if he heard me.

Spinning in Place

Jeff had been waiting to watch the World Cup soccer finals. But at quarter of three on Sunday, during the pregame show, he experienced persistent, severe air hunger.

A nurse and a respiratory technician went to work on him. No matter what they did, Jeff felt as if he were choking. I learned that this was his second panic attack of the day.

He blacked out for a few seconds. When he roused, he said everything was spinning. Everything was scary, he said.

"It felt like I was ... " His words trailed off, the thought unfinished.

The nurse pushed him to finish the sentence: "You felt like what?"

"I felt like I was dying," he said. "Dying. Dying. It felt like I was spinning and dying."

He calmed down. He wanted to watch the game again. The lights were shut off. The room spun again. Jeff started choking again. No matter how well his lungs were actually breathing, in Jeff's mind he was choking, spinning, and dying.

By now, four of the staff were in the room. I was against a wall, sitting in a chair.

"I'm so sorry," Jeff said, ashamed to be the center of so much attention, so much need.

....

A wastebasket full of half-written cards ... confirms that there just aren't words to express how our hearts go out to you. A day doesn't go by that I don't think about you all and hope for the best. There is little we can offer you but time—which I'm sure is becoming more precious each day.—BRUCE TODESCO

....

Karen Zemel, a young doctor with whom Jeffrey had fallen somewhat in love, spent some time with Toby and me in a small conference room we had commandeered as Galli Central. We talked about famous quadriplegics—Chris Reeve and Travis Roy. I said, "Offering them up as examples to quads is like offering Tom Cruise as an example of a typical young man in America."

We talked about religion, just a bit. And we talked about memories and how quads can make them. We talked about how hard it was to envision a good life for Jeffrey, especially as his parents aged and dropped away.

Karen told us the trick was to hope that there would always be people who would care about Jeff and who would want to take care of him. Without knowing, we must expect it, she said.

When he woke from a short nap, Jeff was proud to say he was not having air hunger anymore. I told him he didn't need to be ashamed when he did have it. It was a feeling that was real, not imagined out of fear. "Air hunger is a feeling that comes from air traveling through your throat and lungs in ways it didn't before. It's not your fault."

He said he understood.

He said he wanted to be rotated and asked me to turn on the motor so that the bed would swing slowly from side to side. I asked him if it felt good, like rocking in a cradle.

No, he said, it felt bad. But if it would help with the circulation of his blood, he wanted to do it. He wanted to do whatever he could to get better.

He asked where he would go to school in the fall. Could

he go back to East Greenwich High School? We started to tell him about complications between a months-long rehab and the start of school in September, but he cut in.

"Will I have to go to a school for cripples?"

Good Old Times

Jeff got a visit from Gary and Jan St. Peter. Gary kept talking about an old photo he said they had of Jan and Toby, sitting on a couch, each of them nursing her firstborn: Jeffrey Galli and Chris St. Peter.

Jeff and the St. Peters reminisced about a trip years before to Vail. Jeff had tagged along on a St. Peter family vacation. Jeff was just a tyke. He was still using skis back then. Now Jeff was saying over and over that Matt St. Peter (Chris's younger brother) must try snowboarding. It was exhilarating—Jeff used that word—to lean into a turn, cutting it tight.

When Jeff and Gary swapped memories of their "great moments," there was a brilliance in Jeff's smile that outshone all the gauges in the darkened room.

It broke my heart to watch it. As Jeff made slow, tormented progress trying to salvage his ruined capacities, he would know that his best memories of life had all been set in time already. This other family had given Jeff bits of memory that—no one knew it at the time—would have to last forever as among the best, the very best.

Jeff once owned a hat he almost always wore. It was a fitted Chicago Bulls cap. He lost it during the trip to Vail.

At a restaurant he saw his hat—he was *sure* it was his hat —on the head of a very tall and muscular man standing in a line.

Jeff was sure no one else at Vail could possibly have a hat like that, so he persuaded Gary to approach the man and ask to check inside the hat for Jeff's name. Gary risked his teeth to get Jeff's hat.

Jeff laughed as they retold the story. Gary laughed. We all laughed. Every time the story gets told, the man gets bigger, and the peril to Gary becomes more imminent.

Thirty years from now, when Jeff's peers are remembering three decades of ski trips, and their proms and graduations, and first loves and first loving, and a whole galaxy of transitions and progressions, my Jeff will still be clinging to—and smiling at—the memory of Gary and the guy with the hat.

I was grateful that my friends had given Jeff a memory so strong and happy. But I could not believe the memory could carry so much weight forever. And I could not be satisfied, knowing it might have to.

··················

Please know that I really do care about you and that I wish there was something I could do to ease your pain. I can't tell you that I know how you feel. I only know the sadness that I feel myself.—JUDITH WILSON-DROITCOUR

··················

Half an hour after starting his long sleep for the night, Jeff roused and entered an accelerating round of choking events. He couldn't breathe. Even while his breathing was recording perfectly on the monitor, my boy couldn't breathe. Nurses came and went singly or in pairs, searching for a fix.

They suctioned his mouth and his tracheostomy tube. They disconnected the tube and pumped him with the ambulator bag, while his tube was flushed by a deeper, more rigorous method. He hated it. His throat hurt terribly. He pleaded with them, "No, no, no, no!"

The nurses never ignored his pleading. Each time they had to invade him, they explained the process and won his permission. And so they pushed the plastic tubing down his throat and he squinted his eyes, scrunched his face, and cried his awful, dry-teared cry.

Jeff was apologizing for everything: for jumping in the pool; for being a pain in the butt; for making us spend so many hours in his hospital room; for crying. He asked me to hold him, and I tried to find a purchase on his forehead and cheeks, fitting my fingers around the carbon rods of his halo.

He said he was afraid of dying. He had nightmares about being suctioned.

No matter how often and in what detail we explained to him the ventilating system, he couldn't shake the fear of suffocation. I promised him he would not have to get used to the air hunger. I promised him it would eventually go away. A new kind of tracheostomy tube would help. Getting to the next stage—the rehab hospital—would help even more. He said he was afraid the equipment would break.

"Jeffrey," I said, "the equipment costs fifteen, maybe even sixteen dollars. It's not going to break." His smile, in reaction, was weak.

Finally, the nursing staff and a respiratory technician solved the technical problems. They gave Jeff a bolus of propofol to put him to sleep.

Monday, July 13

....

Nourishment

At one-thirty in the morning on Monday, I walked into
the nearly empty cafeteria alone. I needed something "for-
mal" to eat. I looked back and realized that since the
evening of July 4, I had eaten four meals. One was take-out
Indian food, spooned cold from a cardboard canister four
hours after it was purchased. I had one breakfast: a slice of
sausage and a pancake. I had two suppers of tuna salad on
lettuce, with olives.

Apart from these, over the past eight-plus days I had been
grabbing gulps and handfuls of soda, juice, milk shakes,
cookies, sandwiches, crackers, candy bars—anything that
was hanging around, and the friends who visited made

sure that meant plenty. We were never without food, but we rarely had a meal. I had too much food, but no nourishment.

Jeffrey, on the other hand, had no solid food at all and didn't know if he ever would have any.

....

Stan and I and the girls just want to tell you how much we are thinking of you all and how badly we all feel. We take healthy lives so much for granted. A tragedy such as this affects us all.—BETH WEISS

....

I went to the cafeteria well after midnight not because I was hungry—in fact I was *not* hungry—but because I needed to reconnect with the world of choices and gratification. I could choose a juice or a soda or a coffee milk. The simple exercise of forking some tuna, delivering it to my mouth, and tasting the salt and pepper was —I hated to think it—almost blissful. I knew Jeffrey would never be able to do that. I hated to think he would never do that. Yet it made the bite of tuna taste so much the better.

As I sat in the cafeteria at the end of the day—the beginning, really, of the next—I had in mind that Toby and I had not discussed Option Two for a couple of days.

For more than eight days, Jeffrey's body had been fighting to live, and the hospital staff had been fighting to keep it alive. Toby and I had been convulsed by the notion that we ought to end it for Jeff. In the meantime, our friends had never stopped coming. They came in packs, in squadrons, armed with food and books and videos for Jeff. And we heard about the others, out there, who were praying for us and wishing us well.

Now I felt battered by it all. The compassion—the sheer weight of it—was getting to me. All our friends, and all those people I didn't know, had all bonded together in a common hope: to save Jeff's life. His life. His precious life.

This tragedy had been delivered to us by chance, not politics. The accident had no agenda. For Toby and me, Jeff was the only agenda. Jeffrey was not a flag bearer for any point of view. He was not a poster boy for any cause or class of people. He represented no constituency: not handicap rights, not social or medical policy, not religion. I refused to position Jeffrey into someone else's context.

We were alone in this; we had to be alone and in control. That was the only way to do this right. I kept reminding myself of that. I tried so hard, so long, to believe it.

....

I wish there was something I could do to lessen your pain—
but I know I can't. What I can do is look after and
visit your mom. We had a good visit yesterday—she's quite
strong. We looked at old pictures and her painted china.

—KIM TODER

....

The Meaning of Life

Sitting in the cafeteria early Monday morning, essentially alone, I tried to make peace with my lonesome thoughts.

All around us were people who wanted to save Jeffrey's

life. Whatever their religion, whatever their politics, they all had that in common: they wanted life. That made it difficult. How could his parents oppose life? How could we be so monstrous and so *renegade?*

But what was life, in general? What was life, when considered on its own? People have life, but so do gnats. I had once told Dr. Fritz, "I don't care about Jeff's life. I have no more concern with Jeff's life, in general, than I have for the life of a gnat, in general."

Jeffrey was not a vessel that carried a cargo called life. Jeffrey's life was part of the marvelously complicated matrix that had been Jeffrey before the accident. Now the matrix was less than it had been. Parts of it were missing or broken.

Of the things that remained in the new matrix, Jeffrey's life was still only a part. Only a part. It had no independent significance.

Jeffrey's life derived importance, not from a religious tract or a political thesis, but from its role in enabling Jeffrey. Jeff's life was important to me in direct proportion to its value to Jeffrey.

Rabbi Cahana had said that in traditional Jewish doctrine, life was considered absolutely valuable. As with most religious absolutes, this one seemed to me rationally impoverished. Throw a man in boiling oil and then ask him how "absolutely valuable" it would be to live another hour or two.

There were no absolutes. There was no absolute cure for paralysis; there was no absolute future for Jeff; there was no absolute value to a leg or an arm or a life. The only thing that approached the absolute was that Toby and I had the right and the responsibility to make choices.

In my heart, as I sat alone in the cafeteria, picking at my tuna salad, I still believed that the pain of Jeff's diminishment exceeded the value of living the lesser life of a quadriplegic. The question was, What do I do about that now? Not the day of the accident; not two days later. Now. What do I do about it *now?*

Navigating the River

When I reconnected with Toby in the family lounge later that morning, she raised the subject.

"He wants to live," she said.

"When we started this process," I told her, "we thought we were going to make the decision in private. We thought that you and I—just we two—would make the decision. We were wrong.

"Our friends are involved," I said. "They have taken a personal stake in the outcome. People have started working for Jeffrey. People we don't even know.

"It's like a River," I said, trying to give words to the feeling inside me. During the early hours of Monday morning, the metaphor of a River had begun to form in my mind and had stuck there, becoming a powerful, persistent image that I could not shake.

"Like rudderless boats in a River," I told Toby, "we are being pushed along by the current, seeing the direction in which we are headed but no longer capable of setting the course. We are being driven by momentum."

By the time we had this conversation, I had begun to imagine the exact shape, color, and texture of the River. It had become the great metaphor for my current predicament. I began to see it as a specific thing, nearly a reality. I could see the River's dark water flowing, the sun glinting off the tops of the swells; and I could see a grassy bank and a line of trees in the background.

Everyone around us—doctors, nurses, friends, even strangers who had been struck by our story—had become a tributary or at least a little drop of water. They had all contributed to the River in some way: visits, cards, food, telephone calls, a hug or a pat on the back. And, most of all, their thoughts. So many people thinking about us, all the time. Their thoughts permeated my world like the air itself, like the climate. All of this involvement by friends and strangers, like droplets from melting snow in springtime, had made their way to us, surrounded us, engulfed us, and formed a River—a River of community intent.

To life, it flowed. As if that were the only point on the compass.

And now my family, which I had expected would handle this thing alone, found itself enthralled by that River, having to swim within it. Sometimes I felt the River buoying me up; sometimes I felt myself drowning in it.

A river's current has only one direction. The individual droplets are gentle, but when massed together they are strong, ponderous, and indomitable. Try to move to one side or the other, and the pressure of the current—the overwhelming weight of it, the mass of it—pushes you back in line. I felt as if we were paddling alone, trying to find our way, but all those well-meaning people—those gentle droplets showering down on us as if from a summer storm—were coming together, joining together in a body, and pushing us in the one direction they knew how to flow. It was becoming so hard to consider any other course.

I said to Toby, after a while, "It's like we're waiting to get a sign." She agreed. "I half hope the fever will take him away," she said. Jeff had developed an uncontrollable infection. His temperature was spiking. It could take him away, truly. What she meant was, I wish someone or something else—even more bad luck—would make the decision for us.

We ended our talk Monday morning without resolving anything.

"It's late," I said. "Let's just continue with this job we have to do."

....

Words cannot begin to describe our shock and sadness at learning about Jeffrey's accident. We hope the thoughts, wishes, and prayers of all of us who are fond of all of you will help sustain you in the time ahead. Our hearts ache for you.—VIVIAN WEISMAN.

....

Memorials

In the morning, Jeffrey's intravenous lines were relocated. He had so many fevers, and the antibiotics had not snuffed them out. The staff decided that the fevers were too persistent; that the IV site itself might be the source of the infection; and that a new, clean site might help.

A physical therapist came in later and began showing us how to exercise Jeff's limbs and joints. Without exercise, without stretching, Jeff's ligaments would contract and make claws of his hands and feet.

I watched Toby manipulate Jeff's separate, unresponsive parts.

It was excruciating. As his fingers were flexed and his toes bent back and forth, I paced the room and finally retreated to a corner so that Jeff could not see me.

Jeff apologized for putting everyone to all this effort. Then he said, "I've been thinking of Jimmy."

"Jimmy who?" I asked.

"J. T. Walsh," he said. "I've been thinking of his memorial service."

A few weeks before, a prominent actor (who was a college chum and the brother of a close friend of ours) died suddenly, at the peak of his career. Before his death, Jeff and Sarah had become great fans and liked to watch movies in which he appeared. After Hollywood said its good-byes, a memorial service was held in Rhode Island, where Jim Walsh had spent his young manhood. I was one of the speakers at the service.

Jeff said he remembered my speaking there. That was a chilling thought. Over the past week, I had several times imagined a memorial service for my son. I had imagined what it would be like, standing there in front of our friends, Jeff's friends, and family. Trying to explain how we could have let him go.

Now, I suspected, my son had also been imagining his own memorial.

Toby and I talked again later that day.

"I have never been in a situation where there was no out," I told her. "Before in my life, no matter how tough the situation, there was always something to do. Some objective to achieve. In my professional life, no matter how hard it was, I always had a goal: win the case or settle it. At home, if something broke or leaked, I fixed it or got it fixed. Everything had some kind of purpose."

But now this situation had only two possible outcomes: Jeff would die or he would live trapped in his quadriplegia. I couldn't imagine that, couldn't visualize it.

Toby could. She had lately received a harsher education than I.

Jeff had moved his bowels, and Toby was asked to help two nurses clean him. Because of his unresponsive body and his breathing tubes and equipment, he could not take a bath or shower. Toby and one nurse rolled Jeff onto his side and held him there while the second nurse cleaned him with fluid and thick absorbent pads. Then they had to roll him onto the other side to complete the job.

Toby gagged at the smell and had to leave the room. Later she apologized to the nurses for her weakness. She recognized it as weakness. She knew, more perceptively than I, that Jeff's care would require strength, not just the willingness to be inconvenienced.

I suffered from a failure of imagination. Paralysis was repugnant to my imagination.

"I can't imagine living if we kill our son," I told Toby.

"But I can't imagine living if we let him live. I just can't imagine life, no matter which way this ends.

"Neither result is acceptable to me," I told her. "Neither result is satisfactory."

Later, in a conversation with Gary St. Peter, I put it a bit differently.

"Our family is going to take a casualty," I said. "The only question is whether it's one or two."

Jeffrey received two visitors from school: young girls his age, classmates. The two told him about their summer jobs, the things they were doing, and the places they were going.

The girls laughed, and Jeff smiled and his eyes sparkled. But I noticed that he rarely looked directly at them, rarely let his eyes meet theirs.

I left the room so that they could have a real visit, without the geezer listening in.

The Very Best of All Possible Electric Shavers

Jeff had his first shave since the accident. He asked for it. I ran out and bought an electric razor.

As I began to shave him, I explained each step. I moved slowly. I taught him to pull on his upper lip, to stretch it, so that I could get all of his mustache. He clenched his teeth and stuck out his chin so I could get as much of the underside as possible.

The tracheostomy tube was in the way. One small patch of goatee was out of reach.

Jeff asked me how much the shaver had cost. I told him he didn't want to know.

Getting the razor had been a major project, and an education. I had left the hospital, gotten in the car, and begun to drive. I was completely disoriented. First, I decided to go to a mall but couldn't decide which one. I started going south, then changed my mind and headed north. Then I decided to try the Apex store in Pawtucket. I'd been there a hundred times. I drove a little, made a turn, then second-guessed myself. Took a right at a light, then decided I should have gone left. Stopped along the road to formulate a plan. Drove on again. At an intersection, I sat motionless as the light turned green. Focusing on nothing in particular, I was roused only gradually by the horns honking behind me.

At the store I read box after box to find the right shaver. I would hold two boxes next to each other, comparing each feature, almost every word. I needed a razor that would fit Jeffrey. Fit around his halo bars and tracheostomy tube. Eventually, inevitably, I got the most expensive one they had. If Jeff lives, I thought, he should get the best of everything: best rehab hospital, best life, best shaver.

I told the story to Gary St. Peter. "Can you see it?" I said. "There I am, looking at all these boxes, as if there is *any chance* I'm going to walk out of there with something less than the best." Gary laughed. Sure, as if I were going to try to save twenty dollars on my son today.

When I got back from the store, I told Jeff we could shave him first thing the next morning. But five hours after I said that, he said he could not wait. Just before he settled down for the night, he wanted me to shave him. And I did.

So there we were. Me shaving around his tubes and struts. Him lying rigid as a mummy, except for his face, puckering and twisting to put his whiskers in my path. I don't think it's the shave he really wants, I said to myself. I think it's my touch he really wants.

At least, as Hemingway once wrote, "Isn't it pretty to think so?"

....

Please, Toby, if you need anything I'm only a call away.
I don't want to push myself on you—but if you need
me—just call. I can help with Sarah, food, shopping, etc.
—ABBY LEAVITT

....

Taking It Out on Dr. Fritz, Again

Dr. Fritz, Jeff's psychiatrist, had another talk with me. Fritz was definitely in Jeff's corner. He could not imagine anyone choosing to terminate Jeff's life support. "Everyone seems to agree with you," I said. "They all expect Jeffrey to be saved."

"That's what God would want to happen," Dr. Fritz said.

"We don't mention that name in this room," I warned him.

Fritz and I had another theoretical debate over whether parents have the right to terminate their child without the child's consent. This was old stuff by now. This discussion had been refined during so many hours, with so many people, that poor Dr. Fritz was pretty much KO'd in the early rounds. Of course, bound by the rules of his profession, he might have been pulling his punches.

"There's no question Jeff wants to live," I said at one point. "It is in the nature of living things that they want to continue living. It's programmed into Jeff, and you, and me. No one wants to die.

"But Jeff's life is part of a package. Life has no independent value to me, apart from the person who is living it. I don't want to hear from anyone who believes in the absolute value of life as an abstract or independent thing. There are no absolutes. As difficult as the job may be, everything has to be evaluated. Even life. Whatever that is.

"As a lawyer," I told him, "I am used to working with burdens of proof. In a criminal prosecution, the state has to prove its case beyond a reasonable doubt. In this case, if I propose the death of my son, shouldn't the burden on me be at least as great as it would be in court? Shouldn't I have to be convincing beyond a reasonable doubt that my son should die?

"Or is it enough," I asked him, "that I say, 'I am his dad. I *know*'?"

I was feeling a bit malevolent.

"You know, chance got us here," I told Dr. Fritz. "Why not let chance decide the outcome?" It was clear Dr. Fritz didn't know what I was talking about. So I told him.

"I have wondered if we should just flip a coin," I said, "and let chance decide. Heads he lives; tails he dies."

Dr. Fritz grimaced.

"Or maybe," I said, "that's how I'll decide my own position, and once the coin flip has decided it, I'll argue that way to the end."

"You couldn't do that," Fritz said.

"How do you know," I replied. *"Maybe I've already done it."*

After a while I recognized that I was having this conversation only because it woke me up; I was tired, my mood was down and I needed the stimulation. I felt I ought to end it.

I told Dr. Fritz more about the River. I told him what it had been like, trying to paddle against the current. I told him the River had done its work: we were stuck on course, and we were unlikely to terminate our son's life without Jeff's consent. We had waited too long for that.

He didn't need to worry, I said. I could tell him how this thing was going to turn out.

The River would keep pushing us toward life. And we would go along. At some point Jeff would be ready to talk about it, and we would raise the issue. And he would choose life. And we would support his choice.

At that point I started to sound like a clip from *Casablanca:* "Some day," I said, "maybe not now, but some day, and for the rest of our lives, we will regret it."

Confirmation

The doctor who had approached me the day after we met the ethics committee came to see me again. He had performed his "due diligence." Yes, he assured me, if after Jeffrey becomes an adult he were to choose to withdraw his own life support, Jeffrey would be accepted into a medical service, and his wish would be carried out.

I thanked him. I also told him that our position had been changed in the past few days. Whereas at first Toby and I had been willing to make the decision without informing Jeff—without terrifying him—he had grown into his situation and was now capable, and so we would not go the final step without talking to Jeff about it.

LATER THAT DAY I had a discussion with Dr. Duncan. He was pleased with Jeff's progress and his spirits. It was time to start moving him to the next level, Duncan said. We should pick a rehab hospital and get on with it.

I asked him to tell me what would happen to us. I was worried that there was too little left for Jeffrey to rehabilitate. I was worried that his parents didn't have the youth or the strength to keep Jeffrey at home very long and provide him with a life worth living. I asked Duncan how many kids like Jeff, with injuries as high and as severe as Jeff's, went home to their parents. He said he did not know. I asked him how much of a database there was for cases like Jeff's. Dr. Duncan said there wasn't much.

"But," he told me, "you didn't ask me for statistics. You asked me about Jeff. We know him now. We know his parents now. You will find a way to make it happen."

Basic Training

Just before Jeffrey went to sleep, he asked again, "What's going to happen to me?"

"So you want to run through the chronology again?" I asked.

"Sure," he said.

And so I did: "You rest here and begin to heal your fractured neck bones. You get stabilized. Then to the rehab hospital. You get trained and fitted. We get trained as well. Then you come back to our house, or to a new house, or to somewhere else."

"I don't want you to have to get another house," he said.

"It's not a problem," I said. "A house is just bricks and mortar and lumber and pipes. I don't care if we move or not. It's too early to tell."

Jeff was still anxious about what he would be doing, and so I said, "When I went into the army, I didn't know what I would be doing. That's why they have basic training. They tested me and figured out what I could do and what I could be trained to do.

"Now you've been drafted," I told Jeff. "You'll go to basic training at the rehab hospital, and that's where we'll decide what to do next. They'll test you and train you, and train us, and we'll find out what to do next."

That seemed to satisfy Jeff, and he settled down for the night. I didn't tell him the rest of the analogy. After basic training, they send you to war.

....

I remember you well from early childhood and the
way we all once were. I wish so hard that you can con-
tinue to enjoy life as fully and actively as you did
when we were four. I hope you can draw even a small
amount of comfort from the words of one of your
first friends. Remember that in every crevice of life
people love you and are pulling for you.

—ELISABETH KOSTERLITZ

....

Tuesday, July 14

....

IN THE MORNING, JEFFREY ADDED TO HIS LIST OF SELF-recriminations.

"If only I had not brought my bathing suit to the party," he said.

The "if onlys" are the terrible, inevitable result of chance on a rampage. An accident like Jeff's is the product of an infinite number of variables, any one of which could have changed the result: Was the water level too low? Was the bottom of the pool built too shallow? Did Jeff jump too high? Was he a pound too heavy or an inch too trim? Was the slope of the pool's bottom wrong? Should there have been signs posted? Why didn't it rain that day? Why did he stop playing badminton? Why didn't he eat another brownie? If he had driven a mile an hour more slowly, would we have gotten there a minute later, and would that have made a difference?

Everything counts, but nothing will change. Jeff doesn't get a chance to do it over again. He can make his list of "if onlys" as long as he can bear to make it. He can identify every variable that, if varied, might not have ruined him. It can be a very long list. He has the time.

Boys Will Be Boys

In the evening, Gary and Matt St. Peter came to visit. They were with Jeff more than half an hour while I was busy somewhere else. As I approached the room, I could hear the sound of laughter from thirty feet away.

As I entered the room, there was a hush in the conversation. A conspiratorial hush. I could have been a nurse—or worse, a mom. As the conversation gradually resumed, I realized Gary and his younger son had been talking to Jeffrey about a local *strip joint*.

I didn't know what Gary had in common with nude exotic dancers and my boy, but what a flame was burning in that room!

It became clear, gradually, that Gary, Jeff, and Matt had been planning a great escape. They had decided it would be a good idea to take Jeffrey out for a man's breakfast one day soon. The local strip joint called it "legs and eggs." The three of them weren't sure if they should lower Jeff from the window—it was only three or four stories—or assemble a commando team and orchestrate diversions. They were trying to decide which of the nurses should be taken as helper-hostages. It was a fantasy, and a fantastic one.

Then they began reliving old times—times together, but also their own separate memories of childhood and boyhood. Like a string of firecrackers, memory after memory began to pop. We all joined in. It was a boys-will-be-boys fiesta. In our separate ways, we had all been crazy kids. In our separate ways, we had all kicked chance in the butt.

A friend had taught Matt to bet on horses when he was five years old. Now he was learning to pilot an airplane. Imagine that. A kid who risked a few of his old man's dollars and flew a plane less powerful than the family sedan I drove to the hospital. Big deal.

Jeff once killed a beetle with my air gun, a target pistol. The beetle was huge, and the first pellet ricocheted off its wings. Gosh. And maybe if the geometry had been exactly right, and the wind not too strong or too weak, a pellet from that underpowered pistol might have bounced back at Jeff and given him a startle.

I used to go out on a lake with some friends, in a little boat. We would put firecrackers down the throats of sunfish —a hateful breed—and throw them straight up in the air, showering ourselves with scales and innards. Now we were getting somewhere.

Gary let his future wife's sister ignite one of Gary's farts in his future wife's parents' living room, while his future father-in-law howled with laughter. Funny, but not terribly adventurous.

Jeff had bungee-jumped on a family vacation to Mexico the year before. Big deal. Real adventure does not include waiting on line for your turn.

Matt had just returned from rock climbing in Oregon. Not bad. He practiced by climbing the exterior of his and a neighbor's house and two or three stories up the side of his father's office building. Not bad at all.

I had built a cannon out of a hardened steel pipe. It made the loudest sound I had ever heard and shredded a phone book with a single, tiny BB. That was interesting!

Gary and his friends would hang from a railroad trestle, and as the train roared below them, they would drop into open freighters of sawdust, having no idea what lay under the surface. Five miles down the track, while the train was still moving, they would jump off and catch a bus home. That was really good. Not only was it hazardous, but they did it more than once.

While building one of my adolescent bombs in my bedroom, I ignited my whole cache of explosive powder, splattering with shrapnel my bedroom wall, my shirt, and my chest, and causing my ears to ring so loudly that I could not hear my parents screaming from downstairs. That was best of all! A really dangerous explosion, wounds, and hysterical parents. An unbeatable combination. I won.

We let it all out. What a validation. What a revelation. What a release. We talked about things that made us feel loose and reckless and uninhibited and loony.

We talked about the crazy, wild, insane, carefree, dangerous, lethal, incendiary things that young men do, have done, will always do, *when their parents are not looking.* And please note well: there was no way our kids could compete with Gary and me, the two middle-aged guys with mortgages.

If paralysis is the price Jeff paid just for jumping into a swimming pool, then Gary should long ago have been a bunch of broken bones in the bottom of a hopper, and I should have been a smoking cinder.

Gary and I connected with our boys at their level; we didn't ask them to come up to ours. We left behind our aging metabolisms, our numbing responsibilities, and our damnable sense of prudence. With our boys, we returned to an earlier, younger life when the world didn't scare us so much. The four of us swapped favorite stories, favorite movies, favorite jokes. Jeffrey found the vigor he needed to keep pace. When Jeffrey spoke, his excitement pushed past the tracheostomy tube, and his voice—muscled by enjoyment—was strong and full of personality.

The more we talked, the louder we became. It was as if Jeff and I were sprinting to keep up with Gary and Matt; we were being spurred to a higher level of glee. Jeff should have been exhausted from the effort. In fact, I could see from his monitor that his heartbeat was erratic. But so was mine. For two solid hours, my boy was having fun. Maybe not new fun. Maybe only the joy of remembrance. But after all the recent horror, fun of any kind was delicious. He sparkled.

Suddenly, I had an idea. At first I repressed it. It caught in my gullet. But I couldn't keep it in. I had to let it out.

"You know," I said, "I think we should all agree to get together again on July 4, 1999. We should all agree to get together again and set off some kind of explosion."

What a great idea! It was unanimous. There would maybe be a rocket, or maybe a radio-controlled kamikaze airplane, and certainly something filled with gasoline. Everyone had ideas. Gary, for example, wanted something with a MIRV capability: multiple warheads. I preferred something more simple, less likely to fail, but with a really big flame. "I know someone who owns a gravel pit," I said. "He might let us use that for a location . . . " I had visions of the noise, the flame, the excitement, even the police . . .

As I heard myself planning this awesome prank, I knew that I had invited my son to live long enough to set it off.

After the Laughs

Gary suggested we wrap it up just seconds before the nurse came in to shut us down. He and Matt said their good-byes, promising to be back frequently. After they left, time settled back into its listless rhythm, the minutes stopped crackling, and Jeff started to confront again the reality of his situation.

A new episode of agony began.

Jeffrey decided that he would move his fingers. He just decided to do it. He willed his fingers to move. He *was* moving his fingers! He was *sure* they were moving.

"Look at them," he told me. "Look at the fingers on my right hand. They aren't moving much, maybe just a millimeter."

He *knew* they were moving, if only a little. He said he could *feel* his fingers gently touch the sheet, then lift off a little bit, then drop down and touch the sheet again.

As he said this, I was holding his right hand in my hand. He couldn't see me holding his hand because his eyes were pointed at the ceiling. His fingers were warm, but that was all. In his mind, the fingers were certainly moving. In the real world, they were dead calm.

That, my son, is paralysis.

But nothing could stop Jeff now. He was set upon a frantic, delusional search to find something—anything— in which some fragment of feeling or movement had returned. He closed his eyes, gritted his teeth, and tried his very best. He fought against his injury with the only tools his injury had left him: the best parts, his head and his heart.

They weren't enough.

Jeffrey's head was shaking as if with malaria. His eyes were closed tightly. His face was flush and red with the strain. He was absolutely, resolutely determined to move. Russian weight lifters have grimaces that approach the intensity of Jeffrey's. Women in labor have faces almost as contorted as his. As his muscular body lay motionless on the bed, Jeff's neck and face nearly burst with the effort to move something, somewhere, anything, anywhere. And nothing moved. Not anything. Not anywhere.

"I'm going to cry," he said.

"Go ahead," I told him. "Go ahead and do it. You deserve it."

But he fought it. His teeth chattered. They clicked. He seemed like a volcano of desolation about to explode.

"It feels like I'm sinking," he said.

"Sinking where?" I asked.

"When I close my eyes, it seems like I'm sinking into the floor."

After a while his face relaxed just a little. His jaw became less set; his teeth didn't knock. His strength wilted. His effort died. He sagged.

Wanting More

I knew why the convulsion had overcome him. With Gary and Matt, Jeff had just experienced the best two hours of his last two weeks. Because he had needed a release so badly, it was possibly the best two hours of his life. And he wanted more. He wanted it so much he was finding the will to fight, struggle, battle, scratch, do anything to have more. More elation. More laughter. More memory. Another joke. Another breath with which to purchase it.

In time I talked him gradually into a quieter repose. I told him that he shouldn't hurt himself straining to do what can't be done, but that it was a good idea to take an inventory of his body parts from time to time, since he would be the first to know of any improvement. "The doctors will be happy if you prove them wrong," I said.

AS I TALKED my son to sleep at 11:32 P.M. on July 14, 1998, the River closed over me, and I was swept away. All the hopes of our friends, the prayers of the faithful, and even the illogical convictions of the uninformed—all of them, like droplets, weighing nothing alone, but together as massive as the Mississippi, pulled me under. Like a leaded corpse, the part of me that had argued so passionately for death was swept downstream and under.

It was Jeffrey's life. It was his fight to fight. He had shown me he wanted to fight, and how hard. It was his fight to lose, if it came to that. It was not my fight to quit.

"I'm glad I didn't die," Jeff said to me.

I stroked his hair. "So am I," I said.

His eyes, moist from tears, eventually closed for the night. I hoped he was lucky in his dreams.

HE HAD STRUGGLED so hard that night. His will was so strong, so intense, so focused. He deserved to prevail, but he did not. On that night, there would be no miracle cure. There would be nothing to reward him for the effort, nothing to satisfy the need.

Chance, which had put him in that bed, had no remorse and never would have any.

Coda

······························

I HAVE SAID THAT MY FAMILY'S TRAGEDY STIRRED THE compassion of my community. I should also say that ours is not the greatest tragedy imaginable. I have spent time in a country where the cities were teeming with people of all ages, missing arms and legs and eyes. All around us are victims of disease and terrible accidents. In my brief stay at Hasbro Children's Hospital, I saw three hearses. I didn't ask why.

The point of writing this story was not to elevate Jeffrey's predicament to something supernatural. Accidents are, by their nature, entirely natural, and Jeff's predicament is not the worst a person could find without much searching.

No matter how bad our situation may seem, I know that there are thousands of families whose situations are so desperate that they would gladly trade for ours.

I also know that our situation is far from hopeless. As I have said to friends from time to time, the invasion of Normandy and the preservation of our civilization were accomplished by people who were, by and large, average. I think we can handle this.

SOMETIMES I THINK our fates—Jeff's and mine—were sealed at the side of the pool, as I looked into his empty eyes and resolved to bring him back to life. He was so close to an easy death then; he was almost all the way there.

As I pulled him out, he pulled me in. We met and were transfixed, in a between-world. We are there still.

AT THE BEGINNING of this story, I said that I tried to find a way to kill my son. That is not hyperbole; it is true. For almost ten days—especially in the first few days—I was a strong advocate for Jeffrey's death, and I was a skilled rhetorician. I dealt with everyone, every individual, as well as I needed to. I convinced some, and I neutralized others. When dealing with those I could not convince, I made it possible for them to abstain in good conscience.

THIS WAS NOT the story of Jeffrey's battle against paralysis. That story has just begun. This was the story of Jeffrey's battle against death, and that battle he has so far won. He has so far overcome all of the obstacles he had to face. The world is complicated and risky, and sometimes it appears to be cruel. In this life of chance, of good and bad luck, Jeffrey has overcome risks that millions of other children of his generation have succumbed to.

He made it through gestation, childbirth, and the hazards of infancy.

He avoided auto accidents, drive-by shootings, AIDS, and teenage suicide.

He did not go to war.

He did not starve.

He was not a victim of an epidemic or an ethnic cleansing.

He did not fall off a horse or a rooftop or a ladder.

Jeff didn't drown at the bottom of the pool, and he didn't die on the concrete apron.

At the hospital, he survived shock, infection, and high fevers. His vital organs didn't fail, and neither did his mechanical lungs.

In his desperate, admirable fight for life, Jeffrey pushed through every barrier and turned back every threat. In the end he even managed to push aside the only force that was actually strong enough—or weak enough—to kill him: his dad.

Postscript

....

SHORTLY AFTER THIS STORY ENDED, JEFFREY GALLI WAS transferred from the Hasbro Children's Hospital to a rehabilitation facility in Georgia. A few weeks later, Jeff came back to Hasbro briefly and then spent several more weeks in a hospital in Boston.

In November 1998, Jeffrey came home to the saltbox colonial on Cindyann Drive. He was carried over the brick path (soon to be covered by a new metal ramp) and into the former living room, where an electric hoist would be installed. As the ambulance attendants lowered Jeffrey onto his air mattress, Jeff's mom smiled and Kirby jumped up and licked his face.

Jeff returned to high school in January 1999. Within a few months, Jeff was able to surf the Net, listen to music, do homework, and operate his television using a wireless microphone and voice-recognition software. He began communicating actively by telephone and by using E-mail. His new powered wheelchair arrived in May.

In June the basketball hoop was taken out of its boxes and erected. Sarah sank the first shot she put up.

Because it was important to keep those promises that were within our power, on July 4, 1999, our family and others—including the St. Peters and the Goldsteins—got together and set off two explosions. One was from a cannon I had bought. The other was from a cannon I had made out of hardened iron pipe. After the explosions were over, the homemade cannon was thrown away. It was important to set it off once, but more than that would have been pressing our luck.

Acknowledgments

....

To Wilbur L. Doctor, my first and best teacher of journalism, who helped get me started in a brief career as a newspaper reporter. He preached an old-time newsman's gospel: tell the truth in an interesting way.

To my family: Toby, Jeffrey, and Sarah, who sacrificed their privacy so that I could tell this story.

To the editors who improved the story: Hilary Horton at the *Providence Journal*, Wendy Sherman (my agent), and Antonia Fusco and Rachel Careau of Algonquin Books.

And to the professionals of the Barrington Rescue Squad, Rhode Island Hospital, and the Hasbro Children's Hospital, who gave all of us the first ten days.

Contact Information

....

TO LEARN MORE ABOUT JEFFREY, ABOUT SPINAL CORD injuries, and about some of the technology available to deal with them, you can visit his Web site at http://www.gallicentral.com/jeffhome.htm.

At the site you will find photographs, links to vendor sites and spinal cord injury organizations, a discussion group, and links through which you can contact Jeff by E-mail. He would be happy to hear from you.

You can contact the Jeffrey Galli Trust Fund at PO Box 957, East Greenwich, Rhode Island 02818.